Marriage
& the Spirituality of
Intimacy

Leif Kehrwald

ST. ANTHONY MESSENGER PRESS
Cincinnati, Ohio

Cover illustration by Julie Baker
Book design by Mary Alfieri
Electronic pagination and format by Sandra Digman

ISBN 0-86716-253-8

Published by St. Anthony Messenger Press
Printed in the U.S.A.

For RENE
my best friend,
my beloved,
my partner,
my companion on the journey

Contents

Acknowledgments

I am indebted to the many couples who shared their journey with me. Without their honesty and inspiration, this book would not be possible. The names of all persons (except for my wife, Rene) have been changed or omitted for the sake of privacy.

I am also grateful for the many other couples I have known throughout the years who have modeled healthy, loving and spiritual marriage. I could not have written a book on marriage without their influence; more importantly, I could not have remained happily married for seventeen years without them.

I owe my gratitude to my editor, Carol Luebering, and all the staff at St. Anthony Messenger Press. Through encouragement, patience, critical and creative suggestions, they have made me appear to be a better writer than I actually am.

Finally, I am grateful to Rene, my beloved wife, for her support, critique and helpful insights throughout the writing of this book. Her thoughts and ideas are reflected in every chapter.

Presence: Defining Spirituality in Marriage

She was angry, depressed and exhausted. She was tired of being taken for granted, tired of working without recognition and tired of being ignored. She felt worse than Cinderella. Overwhelmed by it all, she threw the washcloth into the kitchen sink, ran to the bedroom, slammed the door and collapsed in tears on the bed.

Exhaustion and depression were twin demons. They fueled each other and could seemingly pull her into their grip at will. She wasn't just tired; she was *exhausted* to the bone. For weeks no appreciation or affirmation had recharged her batteries. She wasn't just melancholy; she was *depressed.* Never had she felt so isolated and alone.

A short while later he slipped into the room. She had her back to him, and he came up behind her and laid a gentle hand on her shoulder. With a jerk she rejected it. The message was clear: "Don't touch me!"

But after a few moments he laid his hand there again; gently, surely. Sometimes love and remorse are best expressed in silent presence. Neither one moved for long moments. In the prolonged silence he felt her shoulders relax, if only slightly.

He risked further by rubbing them gently. She was about to jerk again, but his touch was soothing. Tension was draining away, so she allowed him to rub. "I'm still mad, really mad," she thought to herself.

The silence hung for a long time. He knew her anger was justified. Indeed, he had taken her for granted and basically ignored her for weeks, all the while expecting everything to be just right at home, especially since his own job had recently been so stressful.

He also knew she would rather be alone with her anger and tears. Yet somehow he knew that, for the sake of their marriage, his presence was paramount. Something told him to remain even though she didn't want him there right now. Something told him to show her in a silent, firm way that he was finally hearing her cries. Something told him that at this moment the totality of their marriage was all rolled up in presence. Somehow he knew that this is the only way they might find reconciliation.

After many long minutes, she finally turned to him with red eyes and tear-stained cheeks. He offered a weak, apologetic grin. Both knew that they could now reconcile; that they could begin to talk through the problem and find a solution. But more importantly, both had a strong feeling they had just been guided through a potentially dangerous experience and had somehow been saved.

Defining Spirituality

A concrete definition of spirituality is so elusive. How can you define something intangible that you know is real?

Down through the ages, traditional Christianity has offered several skewed explanations of spirituality. For some, it refers to what the "specialists" in Christianity do: how monks, nuns and priests pursue a life-style of holiness by removing themselves from the distractions, chaos and temptations of "regular" life.

Spirituality has also suggested a split between the spirit and the flesh, implying that you must choose one over the other. If you seek a spiritual life you must forego the life of the flesh. Would a spirituality of marriage then imply abstaining from making love rather than becoming good at it?

For some, spirituality has been limited to one's inner attitudes, the purity of private emotions. Only a few are called to an interior life with Christ, completely absorbed by his presence, and the term *spiritual* is reserved solely for these mystics.

None of these approaches to spirituality offers much for the majority of believers: those of us who cannot forsake the distractions of life "in the world," who have chosen the "life of the flesh"—marriage—and certainly wouldn't count ourselves among the elite chosen who are infused with the interior light of Christ. Is *spirituality* an exclusive or inclusive term?

In their book, *Marrying Well: Stages on the Journey of Christian Marriage*, James and Evelyn Whitehead offer some hopeful insight about the word *spirituality*.

> If we are to rescue this term and make it vital again we will have to link Christian vision with practical, effective performance of this vision. A contemporary spirituality of Christian marriage will explore the different ways that Christians have envisioned married life, sexuality and religious fruitfulness....
> Such a spirituality addresses practical aspects of life— how we spend our time, how much we work, how and when we worship and play and make love.

Now I feel included. As a believer, I worship, I pray and I make love. When we talk about a spirituality that is manifested in the activities and choices which form my identity—work, family, play and so on—then I am ready to listen and learn with the hope of growing in my faith.

The essence of spirituality is presence: recognizing and responding to the real but unseen presence of God. Sometimes our lives must come to a crashing halt in order to find that presence. Other times it sweeps us up—overwhelms us—right in the middle of our mundane lives. Still other times, the presence seeps into our being almost unnoticed until we are confronted with a challenge requiring uncommon, even heroic courage and strength.

Spirituality may be difficult to pinpoint, but presence bonds us in relationship and gives us strength and courage that we would not otherwise have. Each of us is fully human;

presence makes us more than merely human.

Spiritual means presence—the gentle, but firm presence of a husband to his angry, depressed wife; the persistent though silent presence of God in all aspects of our lives. Spirituality is our response to God's presence. When it makes a difference in our choices and actions, it is an active spirituality.

In marriage, nearly every decision and daily activity is colored by our life-commitment and the current state of our relationship. So, too, with spirituality: Our life-posture is shaped by our commitment to and current relationship with the real but unseen God.

This book is not about a one-and-only spirituality of marriage. Rather, it seeks to break open the possibility of a unique spirituality for any couple who seek to respond to God's presence in their lives. I'm no spiritual mystic, to be sure—just ask my two sons! But with Rene, my beloved, I'm on a journey, a spiritual journey that seeks to connect the regular stuff of our marriage with God's gracious presence.

Marriage can be deeply spiritual simply because its facets touch the core of one's being. Marriage is our posture toward and response to intimacy, conflict, personality, friendship, play, work, health, love, nurturing, sex, faith and so on.

These are the arenas in which spirituality can emerge and flourish, infusing a rich texture to the fabric of marriage. This does not mean the two of us live monastic-style lives, far removed from the frenetic noise and chaos of typical household family life. Not at all! If your life is like mine, moments of uninterrupted solitude are a rare and welcome luxury. My family, my work, my play, my responsibilities all dictate against frequent and prolonged periods of quiet contemplation. Yet God is still present and active.

In marriage there are, I hope, times when you lose yourself in the presence of the other. When engaged together in meaningful conversation, spirited recreation, intimate lovemaking or tearful reconciliation, there is nothing but right here, right now, with her or with him. These are rich moments in and of themselves, but they are also spiritual windows.

God is just as present in the creases and folds of our hectic lives as in church on Sunday morning. When you think about it, God doesn't distinguish between sacred and secular as we do. We tend to consider things connected to Church and religious life as inherently holy, while events connected to home and family as—well, just regular stuff. Not so from God's viewpoint. To the Creator of all, it's all precious and holy and sacred.

Yet we need to recognize that God's presence is *different* at home and in marriage—and that is OK. In fact, it's better than OK, because then we broaden our understanding of who God is in our lives. When we realize the richness of God's presence in marriage, then we begin to realize what a powerful source for practical spiritual growth we have right there in our daily life partner.

With this book I would like to explore the potential for spiritual intimacy in marriage. God seeks to join us in our most intimate encounters—not to meddle or judge, but to foster and enrich our love for each other and to bring us into an embrace of ultimate and lasting love. By that embrace I am empowered in all my life roles—worker, father, teacher and, most especially, husband.

Sounds a bit idealistic, I know. I can already hear Rene chuckling as she reads these words because she knows me all too well, and of course she knows the ups and downs of our marriage. While she won't question my sincerity in attempting to address this worthy topic, she will certainly question our "expertise" as a spiritual couple.

Do we kneel at our bed each evening or morning to pray? Nope. Do we have daily discussions about our prayer life or about God's will for, as an example, how I should spend my afternoon with the kids? Sorry. Do we always and faithfully turn to God in our moments of doubt, struggle and crisis? Usually, but not always. Are the Kehrwalds secretly breaking new ground in their spiritual journey as a couple? 'Fraid not.

Whatever doubts Rene has (or you) about our expertise are well-founded. We're not the spiritual-guru couple. Yet, the desire and sincerity is there. Let's journey together through these pages with the belief that by the end perhaps we will both have taken a step or two toward a richer couple spirituality.

Fortunately, this book is not based solely on the experiences of Leif and Rene. You'll be introduced to a number of couples who are also on the journey and who have been gracious enough to share with me their stories of success and struggle.

Join me, if you will, to explore the spirituality of marriage. Share what you like with your beloved, and disregard the rest. May we both grow in love for our spouses, and may we grow closer to the One who loves us all.

For Reflection and Discussion

- *In your own words, how would you describe or define spirituality? How would you describe your spirituality? Your relationship with the real but unseen God?*

- *How would you describe your spiritual relationship in marriage?*

PART ONE

The Four Postures of Marriage

Spirituality and healthy marriage are linked. When we pursue the spiritual aspects of our relationship, we will surely enhance the overall quality of our love. Similarly, when we seek to enrich the many and varied facets of our marriage, it becomes easier to explore the spiritual realm.

This is not to say that only stellar marriages are capable of deep spiritual intimacy. The story with which we began gives a glimpse of the sacred possibilities in working through hurts. Our pain, even our shortcomings can lead to deep spiritual intimacy, just as the experiences and passages of our lives— the birth of children, career changes, financial troubles, retirement and so on—reveal God's gracious activity. We will explore these ideas in Part Two.

It would be absurd to program in marital struggle just for the sake of spiritual growth (as if what already occurs isn't enough). It makes better sense to focus on our strengths, knowing that these can also enrich our spirituality. I would like to describe four key "postures" that I believe embody a healthy marriage today. These convictions also present unique channels for spiritual growth that I will attempt to describe.

1) *Mutuality:* Mutuality is not the same as equality. Equality implies sameness, while mutuality involves honoring and cherishing differences. Obviously, spouses are different from one another in thousands of ways beyond their maleness or femaleness. Mutuality in marriage implies regarding each other's differences with respect and

1

affording each other equally high integrity for the unique gifts each brings to the marriage. We discover our mutuality in the simple realization of our common humanness, as we will see in Chapter One.

2) *Self-acceptance:* There must be a level of self-love and self-assurance in order to proclaim genuine and lasting love to another. The "yes" you said to your spouse on your wedding day is as rich and deep as your self-love and acceptance. So, gratefully, we are called to say "yes" to each other each day thereafter, thus renewing our opportunity to grow in self-esteem.

3) *Other-acceptance:* The highly charged, romantic euphoria of early love makes one feel as though the other can do no wrong. But when the intense attraction begins to wane, the other's quirks and idiosyncrasies begin to grate. The natural response is to try to change the other, which is always futile. There must come a genuine acceptance of the other, the whole person.

We will delve further into self-acceptance and other-acceptance in Chapter Two.

4) *Openness to growth and change:* As soon as we think we've "arrived" and can coast for awhile, something will surely upset the balance. In many respects you are not the same person your spouse married years ago, nor is he or she the same. Your married relationship has surely evolved into something that only vaguely resembles what you had in the beginning. Change happens. When we can embrace it, we can discover the growth possibilities that come with it, as we will see in Chapter Three.

To me these are the four corners of a healthy marriage. It's important to recognize that these qualities imply conviction and are not just skills to learn. That is, my behavior may at times fall short of the full expression of these beliefs, but all the while my heart remains clear and fixed. These are ideals worth pursuing for a lifetime of marriage. Let's break them open.

CHAPTER ONE

Mutuality in Marriage

Mutuality is richer and deeper than equality because it recognizes the unique character, virtue and giftedness of the other. One tends to think that male and female are created equal. That is true in one sense: All persons, male and female, are equally human. But it is not at all true in the sense that two people in a marriage are the *same* as each other.

In our mutual relationship, therefore, we don't hesitate to explore each other's unique gifts and quirks. We rejoice in the ways our talents, personalities and differences complement each other and contribute to the wholeness that is "us." And, ideally, we do this without regard to gender. We may have been conditioned to follow prescribed gender roles, but we don't really show our true selves until we break out of them.

The masculine qualities in him and the feminine in her may initially attract, but it will likely be the subtle nuances of personality that make the relationship last. Indeed, qualities not typically considered masculine—his warmth, say, or caring and affection—may endear him to her. Similarly, expressions that stretch the boundaries of the feminine may leaven for him a lasting mutual relationship.

Ellen and Doug lead a seemingly traditional marriage and family life. He's an engineer for a major high-tech corporation and she's a stay-at-home mom. They have three children, one in middle school, one in second grade and a preschooler.

From external appearances, their marriage and family life have all the components of a traditional gender-defined household. But that's just the way it looks from the outside. Anyone who knows Doug and Ellen knows that they don't fit the stereotype.

You see, they have a long-standing dream that one day they will own a piece of land in the country, raise a few animals and crops, and live simply and on their own. It's not just a pipe dream. They talk about it constantly, and they're always preparing for the big move. Ellen has been studying the basics of agriculture and looking into raising llamas. Doug frequently takes drives in the country to look at pieces of land for sale. He'll look at just about anything, even if he knows it's not the piece for them, just to stay knowledgeable about the market.

Doug and Ellen are focused together on their dream, and fully support each other's efforts toward achieving it. Therein lies the mutuality of their marriage. While some of the roles they perform now appear rather traditional and might even be construed as sexist by some, this is the last thing Ellen and Doug are concerned about. Doug truly enjoys his work and his colleagues at the office, but, "I'm not a climber like some," he says. "I'm grateful I have skills that earn good money, but I look forward to the time when we can live peacefully off the land. We're saving as much of the money as we can." There is much more to his personhood than his career.

Similarly, Ellen truly loves being at home and finds great fulfillment in her current role, but she can also imagine applying her gifts and skills in a broader realm. "I wouldn't trade my time at home while the kids are growing up for anything, but I'm ready for a bigger plot of land to cultivate than just our little garden."

Ellen and Doug are focused on a journey that they've chosen together. They know they can't get there unless they stay united and supportive of one another. Their mutuality comes from within. They have commingled their dreams into a vision that spurs their energy and imagination—and they are a couple who will pursue their vision with vigor until they attain it. The last thing they are concerned about is stereotypical, hierarchical roles for husband and wife.

The 'Headship' Model

"You can tell who wears the pants in that family." "A man's home is his castle." "You just wait until your father comes home!" "Her 'honey-do' list was a mile long."

Surely you've heard these statements or others like them. They don't exactly show deference to the equality between husbands and wives. Yet, they do reveal the generally accepted attitude in some pockets of society. I believe it takes a conscious, deliberate choice to establish and maintain a mutual marriage relationship in our culture.

Mutuality implies offering full credence and integrity to the characteristics in the other that are different from yours. In contrast, many espouse a hierarchical view of the marriage covenant. This issue arose recently at a presentation I gave at a regional seminary. Several young men had been taught that a man exists on a slightly higher spiritual plane than a woman and therefore carries an extra burden of responsibility for the spiritual welfare of his wife and children. These seminarians were troubled by this and wanted to know my opinion.

Many people believe in the "headship" of the husband over his wife, children and household. He has the ultimate responsibility for their welfare—physically, morally and, most importantly, spiritually. That belief, of course, is considered biblically sound, based on Genesis 2—3 and Ephesians 5, and therefore to be upheld with no question or hint of doubt. Many conclude that "God's plan" for marriage and family living begins with the husband as the spiritual head of the household because he has, in effect, slightly closer access to God "Himself." The wife and children are ever so slightly but assuredly down the hierarchical ladder from him.

I consider this mindset to be the result of cultural blindness at best, and blatant sexism at worst. Throughout history, most cultures of the world have been male-dominated in nearly all aspects of life: politics, business, commerce, government, household living and so on. Religious and spiritual practice is no exception. This culturally conditioned male dominance has given rise throughout history—right up to the present day—to sexist and discriminatory practices that permeate all aspects of society.

Marriage is where women have been hurt the most. The hierarchical spousal relationship has robbed women (and men) of the true and sincere intimacy that all humans crave and need. When a woman is merely the object of her husband's desire and the fulfillment of his needs, is it really possible to sustain a lasting intimacy?

Some may yet ask about the clear biblical command for wives to be submissive to their husbands (see Ephesians 5:22-24). The U.S. Catholic Bishops have addressed this question in their Pastoral Statement on Domestic Violence Against Women, *When I Call for Help*. They state:

> As bishops we condemn the use of the Bible to condone abusive behavior. A correct reading of the Scriptures leads people to a relationship based on mutuality and love.... In Ephesians 5:21-33, for instance, which discusses relationships within the family, the general principle laid down is one of mutual submission between husband and wife. Even when a wife is not abused or treated merely as an object, the hierarchical view cripples her self-esteem and diminishes her personhood.

In *Marriage: Sacrament of Hope and Challenge*, William Roberts offers an insightful interpretation of this passage from Ephesians, recognizing the cultural bias of the time in which it was written. Roberts points out that the societal framework in which Paul wrote these words was that the husband was already the head of his wife. This point was not breaking any new ground at all. What was new and revolutionary to the Ephesians was that husbands were called to "headship" in the same way Christ is the head of the Church. And what does that look like? Complete "servantship." A husband must serve his wife just as Christ gave up his life for the Church. This was completely radical for the Ephesians, who considered their wives to be property.

Remember, Paul was bound by his culture and could not be expected to break entirely out of its understanding of marriage. Yet, from a spiritual and theological viewpoint in our culture today, Paul's message is no less radical.

Roberts states,

> The Christian imperative for marriage can now validly be interpreted in this way:
>
> 1) Wives and husbands must love each other as Christ loves the Church.
>
> 2) Wives and husbands must love each other as they love their own bodies....
>
> 3) Wives and husbands must regard each other as they regard the Lord, responding to each other as fully as possible.

Key to this message, of course, is that both spouses engage in these efforts with mutual enthusiasm. Husband is not on a higher plane than wife, but rather the two are equally and fully human in the eyes of God and should therefore be so in each other's eyes.

Best Friends

Bud and Nancy have developed nontraditional roles in their marriage. Nancy has always been career-oriented and currently works as an executive for a large corporation downtown. Bud is an independent sort who enjoys free-lance writing and primary care of the household. These roles fit them well, for Nancy would go crazy if she had to be home all day with the kids and the house, and Bud could never be content in the corporate commuter crowd.

But like Ellen and Doug, they also have a dream that unites them in a single purpose: hospitality. Bud and Nancy met and fell in love while working as counselors in a group home for troubled teens. The work was exhausting, but they found it extremely rewarding. When they were married, they bought a large house in a "questionable" city neighborhood. "We could have bought something smaller in a better part of town," commented Nancy, "but then we wouldn't have enough room for our guests."

Bud and Nancy have always welcomed less fortunate people into their home and family: a friend going through a bitter divorce, an unwed expectant mother with no means of her own.

"Whoever lives with us becomes part of the family," says Bud. "They take their night at cooking like the rest of us, and they get as much love and support as anyone else."

"Why do we do this?" Nancy explains. "I suppose we would have more money and our lives would be less hectic if we didn't open our doors, but life would also be lacking. This is our charism, our vocation as a couple. Our hospitality to others is a part of who we are as a family. It's not everyone's cup of tea, to be sure, but for us this is right and good."

What Nancy and Bud have in common with Ellen and Doug is a dream, a calling that binds them together and takes them beyond their designated roles. It's a calling that demands mutuality. While far from easy, their dreams constantly put them in touch with each other and force them to look out beyond the immediate struggles or tedium of the day. These couples live mutuality in their marriage.

Mutuality is perhaps the "best friend" part of marriage. In our own deep and true friendship, we don't even see the maleness or femaleness, the feminine or masculine in each other. On a good day, we just see the rich giftedness of the other. On less than stellar days, we too readily see each other's shortcomings.

Our younger son's best friend is a girl. They're both ten years old and have been best friends since first grade. Their play is fascinating to observe. They effortlessly move from building a tree fort to playing with stuffed animals to high-level trade talks over old toys. Theirs is a completely mutual relationship without any prescribed expectations—as though they haven't yet discovered that he's a boy and she's a girl.

Mutuality in marriage involves pure friendship that brings out the best in each other, and leaves expected roles and prescribed behaviors behind.

Human Is Human Is Human

Mutuality means recognizing our common walk in life. What we share as humans far outweighs our differences in gender, personality, upbringing and so on. We are all fully human and fully loved by the Creator. No one is more or less human than the other. Father Jim Galuzzo from Oregon reflects on the human condition this way: "We are all born with an inherent (permanent, essential, intrinsic) human nature which says that all people are connected." In a lecture to a group of parish pastoral ministers on March 19, 1994, he described several characteristics of this inherent human nature.

It is unconditional. There are no conditions, no *if*'s or *should*'s. We are not lovable because we behave a certain way or do certain things. We are simply and unconditionally lovable.

It is whole/complete. Our nature is whole and complete from birth. We don't become more human or less human, more or less good, more or less connected to others. We are everything, always.

Each person lives out his or her inherent human nature in her or his way. This is the beauty of diversity.

Our inherent human nature includes all human qualities that are true for every person. Every woman, every man and every child is inherently good, loving, kind, strong, powerful, creative, intelligent, gentle, sexual, brave, intimate, free, self-healing, lovable, caring, sensual, curious, just, courageous, nurturing and intuitive, to name just a few.

When marriage takes on hierarchical qualities, mutuality is lost and genuine intimacy greatly diminished. Think about it. Is it possible to sustain intimacy with another person when one or the other is believed to be superior? The only way this is possible is for the lesser one to rise momentarily to a higher level or for the greater one to "come down" to meet the other. True and lasting intimacy is mutual, on the same plane.

From God's viewpoint human is human is human—full, complete, whole and totally loved. From God's vantage point intimacy is possible between any two persons simply because they are mutually human, regardless of size, shape, color or gender.

William Roberts puts it this way:

> What constitutes the basic equality of persons is the radical human potential for intelligence, love and free self-determination.... In marriage two persons share that which makes them equal as humans: their minds, their hearts, their free choice to become one with each other.

Mutuality is more than a cornerstone of a healthy marriage relationship. It also carries deep spiritual implications. These implications lie in God's unconditional love for each one of us, which inspires us to love each other and return our love to God.

Spirituality, particularly in marriage, does not remove us from or elevate us beyond the human condition. Rather it immerses us in it, recognizing that being human is the only way we can engage in relationship with each other and with God. From this deeper immersion into our humanity, we discover the sacred nature of our being. In the midst of our faults, failings and shortcomings, we also see the loved and loving creature God has shaped in each of us.

Furthermore, because of our intimate togetherness we can develop a conjugal spirituality: that is, an awakening that is based in and comes directly from our intimate union. In her book, *Conjugal Spirituality: The Primacy of Mutual Love in Christian Tradition*, Mary Anne MacPherson Oliver describes it as "a shift of the center of spiritual attention from within individuals to the spaces between them.... It is a spirituality which looks for the presence and action of God in relationships...and which affirms the couple as a spiritually...significant unit."

Lovers can surely help each other embrace the sacred nature of humanity. Spouses can give spiritual direction to each other. But, as in intimacy, they have to be on the same plane. They must embrace the ideals of mutuality and allow them to permeate all areas of their relationship. Again, like intimacy, true and lasting marriage spirituality is possible only in a relationship of mutuality.

For Reflection and Discussion

- *What does "mutuality in marriage" mean to you? What couples do you know who really live mutuality in their marriage? How?*

- *When have you known your spouse as a best friend? Recall an experience or period in your marriage when one of you really needed pure friendship and understanding.*

CHAPTER TWO

'You're Gonna Like Me'

Years ago Rene and I were youth ministry coordinators at a parish in Spokane, Washington. Each year we took youth group members to the diocesan youth convention: a full weekend of rally, worship, talks and fun. The kids loved it. I get tired just thinking about it.

One year the keynote speaker, a priest from California, gave a great presentation on self-esteem, a perennial issue for many teenagers. During his talk, he conducted a simple icebreaker with the several hundred people in the room. He told everyone to introduce themselves to three people they did not know by saying, "Hi. My name is ____, and you're gonna like me."

His point was simple. Each person is a unique and beautiful creation of God. If you get to know me well enough, sooner or later you can't help but like me. But it's no small thing for any of us, let alone a teenager, to proclaim right out loud that you will surely like what you find in me. It takes some self-assurance. Try it yourself. Go to your beloved, who knows you so well, and say, "Hi. I'm ____, and you're gonna like me." Say it as if you really mean it.

What sort of reaction did you get? Why do you suppose you felt embarrassed? I know, you probably just kept reading and didn't do it. But you can picture yourself feeling embarrassed, right? It probably feels a little arrogant and self-centered to be so sure of yourself. Yet is it self-centered or is it self-grounded?

It all depends on where you place your source of being. If you feel solely and individually responsible for who you are—your personality, your traits and gifts, your place in the world—then perhaps that introduction is a bit presumptive. But if you're grounded in the conviction that every person, yourself included, is God's loved and unique creation and that your talents, traits and personhood are simply an expression of God's grace, then your introduction is wholly appropriate.

This chapter focuses on acceptance: acceptance of self and acceptance of the other, your beloved. What does it take to proclaim genuine and lasting love to another? A sense of self; a sense of sureness. For what is a "yes" proclaimed to another if there is no internal sense of self to back it up?

You could say, then, that one's commitment to another goes only as far as one's internal self-assurance. You can't pledge to another what you don't have. Maybe this is why so many marriages struggle and fail. Yet this is only part of the picture, because the one to whom you pledge your love surely raises your self-esteem. His or her presence in your life empowers you to be more whole.

For example, Rene has always said that before we met, she rarely felt sure about decisions in her life—big or small. She had inordinate difficulty making up her mind about almost everything everything, from choosing which college to attend to selecting an entree from a restaurant menu. But when we met and became friends, she says she could see things more clearly and decisionmaking was not so difficult. A few years later, when we talked of getting married, there was little quandary in her mind and heart. She knew it was the right choice. On the day of our wedding, you should have heard the conviction in her voice as she proclaimed her marriage vow to me. She'll tell you she was completely sure, and that sureness was a grace from God. She still has trouble with a restaurant menu, but her conviction in choosing me as a life partner has not wavered.

Self-acceptance and acceptance of the other are intertwined; each nurtures the other. Our relationship has always strengthened Rene's sense of self, which, in turn has steadily enriched our marriage. Of course, the same is true for me. While I have always been a quick and sure decision-maker, I've realized—recently more than ever—that Rene's presence in my life provides a calming balance that helps me clear my mind and heart. From this posture I can best contribute to my marriage.

The yes you pledged to your beloved on your wedding day was only as rich and deep as your personal self-acceptance at the time. Obviously, the two of you buoyed each other to higher levels during courtship. A true lover brings out the best in the other. As the best of you began to shine brighter than ever before, you were empowered to make a life commitment to the one who tapped your essential goodness.

Unfortunately, we tend to think of the yes on our wedding day as a one-time event. It's a pledge made years ago that we either struggle under or enjoy year after year (or, most likely, some combination of the two).

Yet, we know that marriage is alive and growing. It has a life of its own that requires a yes each and every day, and sometimes several times a day. Each renewal of the pledge is unique, attending a different facet of the relationship that has been exposed and laid vulnerable.

As we mature, so do our challenges and responsibilities. Without personal growth I'm not sure any of us can remain engaged in this dance of love. But of course, marriage is not all challenge and struggle—not at all! The rewards of intimacy, fun and companionship are euphoric and addicting. During the early weeks of our marriage, I couldn't imagine being any closer to Rene than we were then. But each year since I have proven myself wrong. I understand better now that marriage is a lifelong journey. And I am a better person for having chosen this path.

Just think what it will be like after 50 or more years. You're really gonna like me then!

Taking Myself for Granted

My spouse cannot be my only source of strength and support. That is entirely too much of a burden for her. So what am I doing for my own personal growth that will contribute to the growth and freshness of our marriage? What am I doing to enhance my own self-esteem?

Perhaps this isn't true for you but, over time, I begin to take myself for granted. It's easy to assume I continue to exude all those wonderful qualities that Rene was attracted to in the first place: gentle sensitivity and understanding, subtle wit, sincere faith—not to mention dashing good looks and a full head of hair. Yet the skirmishes of life—involving job, kids, cars, house and so on—slowly erode these qualities to the point where I am reduced to only a shell of my former self, one who thinks he still has all those qualities.

It's time for a bit of soul-searching and perhaps some action. Recently, I've tried to reflect on a few questions that challenge me to fill in the shell and recover something of what I once was. I invite you to consider the same questions.

- Is my behavior balanced or addictive? When I consider my basic needs—food, work, intimacy, sex and so on—do these needs control me or do I strike a balance in meeting them? That's what addiction means: my "need" for the substance or issue gains control over my behavior. When I'm addicted I lose my ability to be present to anyone else, even those I love. And when I lose the ability to be present, I lose touch with the sacred. My pursuit of God is thwarted.

- Do I share, or am I selfish? I am actually quite generous when it comes to my things and my time to do stuff, say, around the house: cleaning, cooking, puttering and so on. Yet I find I am increasingly more selfish with my thoughts and feelings. It's not easy to explain my reluctance to open up, but I fear losing touch with my feelings altogether. Again, if I lose emotional touch, there's little opportunity for spiritual growth.

- Do I seek support or isolation? When I'm troubled or burdened, do I crawl into my shell and fend off all my foes by myself, or do I seek support and help from those who are more than willing to lend it? This is a tremendous challenge for me as a stalwart, can-do individualist. Yet I did see a counselor once about a personal family issue, and it was incredibly helpful and freeing. There is help for those who seek it.

- Am I patient or anxious? Can I live within the rhythms and timing of those around me, or do I try to keep things on my timetable? Can I let go of control? There is perhaps no more worthy (or challenging) spiritual practice than abandoning myself to God's timing.

- Am I growing, or am I stagnant? A couple of summers ago I was attempting to teach my sons how to golf. I learned the game at a young age from my father, and always dreamed of teaching my children. Well, I wasn't having much success. They just couldn't get the subtleties of the game that bring positive results. So I decided to become a beginner myself by learning to golf left-handed. While I knew it would be difficult, I had no idea what a challenge it is to learn the golf swing. After several weeks and many buckets of practice balls, I had accomplished very little. So I adjusted my expectations with my sons and then we began to see some improvement. The point here is that in my own learning and growth I became a better teacher and father. Be on the lookout for opportunities to grow. They'll make you a better person.

When I take the time to seriously reflect on these questions, I can think of specific steps I can take to be a more whole person and therefore a better spouse. For example, in recent years I have made (and often broken) these pledges to Rene:

- I will share more feelings from the heart rather than hide behind household tasks.

- I will offer more touch, given freely without expectation of anything in return.

- I will come home from the office less exhausted.

- I will resurrect my dreams and share them with Rene.

What about you? From your reflection are there any pledges you'd like to make to your beloved?

Spirituality of Acceptance

When it comes to self-acceptance, the spiritual implications are deep. By that I mean one's efforts and ability to embrace one's whole self—faults, quirks, gifts, talents, personality— are based on spiritual beliefs.

Self-acceptance must stem from the conviction that I am not my own creation or even my own possession, but rather a gemstone created by God. God has given me the privilege of stewarding the journey of my life. My life is not my own, but God's. Am I a good steward?

This particular idea of stewardship goes against the grain of our culture. We live in a society that is possession-oriented and achievement-driven. All importance is placed on what I can accomplish and accumulate. I am what I do, and what I possess reveals volumes about me. I am a human doing, not a human being.

To say that I am a gemstone created by God and that I fully accept the person I am—complete, whole, gifted, unique— flies in the face of our never-satisfied, always-seeking-improvement society. This is why spirituality is countercultural. It puts the center of being outside myself, in God.

Where is your spiritual grounding? From what do you take your cues? Do you key off external forces, such as society's expectations? Or do you ground yourself in the internal urgings of the Spirit?

To demonstrate the connection between genuine self-esteem and spirituality, try this simple exercise. Bring to mind one deeply spiritual person you know, someone you have encountered in your life who is truly anchored in his or her spirituality. Describe that person in terms of how he or she feels about self and how that person appears to mesh with the rest of society.

I don't know the person you're thinking of, but I have a

hunch you would respond with phrases like this: Seems content and grounded; isn't really in touch with current fads but doesn't seem bothered by that; easy to be with, and yet at the same time challenging; has a sureness that I wish I had; doesn't keep pace with the hustle and bustle of society. Am I close?

My point is simple. When people are rooted spiritually, they have a strong sense of self; they know and embrace both their gifts and their limitations. They don't put a lot of credence in the whims of popular culture. This is not to say they don't care about people. Not at all: They just don't let the ebb and flow of the popular run their lives.

There is a direct link between deep spirituality and genuine self-acceptance. Believing in that which is real but unseen gives each of us more power to believe in ourselves. What about couple spirituality and self-acceptance? As a result of deepening self-acceptance, the depth of one's prayer grows, feeding the spirituality of a relationship. It's a spiral of growth.

Think about it in symbolic terms. Picture a light burning in your heart: your spirituality. Picture the same in the heart of your beloved. Now the stronger those lights burn inside, the easier it is to see the light between you. The source of spirituality is fed from within, but expressed from between the two of you.

The question remains: How do we tap into that source of spirituality and make good use of it in our marriage? That's the key quest of this book, so be patient and keep reading. But the source lies in acceptance—first of self, and then of the other.

Accepting the Other

Ah, accepting the other. I have a friend who, for as long as I've known him, has wanted an intimate relationship in the worst way, but can never find the right match. He's a good man and would be a faithful, devoted life partner but, alas, he has not found the love of his life. I have silently rooted for him in his quest.

Well, my rooting paid off recently. He announced to me he had developed an intimate relationship with a woman about his age (late forties), but while he was beside himself with joy, he had some real questions. Over lunch we talked about how they met, how the relationship had blossomed, the kinds of activities they like to do together and so on. All the while, I was waiting for his questions.

Finally, he came around to his dilemma. He described some interaction between the woman and her young adult children that disturbed him. Apparently, there was a certain amount of verbal abuse that surfaced frequently between them. My friend had not seen this behavior in her before, and was surprised and concerned.

He was asking me if I thought this was something to worry about in their relationship, even though it didn't really involve him. I'm not a therapist or a counselor, and have not received formal training in those disciplines, but it sounded like a red flag to me.

I told my friend that in my opinion people form patterns of relating that are like habits: difficult to break. While the euphoria of courtship may temporarily encourage us to behave differently and better, I said, when we are most relaxed, we tend to revert to habits learned earlier.

We talked about this for quite some time, and I sensed my friend was searching for a way to conclude that the problem was not a problem. He wanted a relationship so badly that he would almost have preferred not to know the struggles and shortcomings of his intimate friend. Yet he had to be honest with himself and realize that she wasn't ready for an intense love relationship.

Even though he's been waiting and hoping his entire adult life, he knows it can't happen without full acceptance of the other. And, in his situation, that means not putting on blinders to hide issues and patterns he'd rather not see. Fully accepting the other is no simple task.

Remember how the highly charged, romantic euphoria of early love made you feel as though the other could do no wrong? Every move he made was a wonder to behold! Every decision she arrived at was a masterful choice! Remember those days? They didn't last long enough, did they? When the intense attractiveness begins to wane, the other's quirks and idiosyncrasies begin to grate. "No big deal," I said to myself, "I'll get her to change soon enough." Ha—seventeen years and still waiting!

I think you'd have to put me in the camp of those who believe that opposites attract. Pilers go for filers. Couch potatoes are drawn to jocks. Punctuals are enamored of the laid-back late ones, and spenders somehow latch onto savers. We are attracted to the qualities in another that we do not possess, and yet these are the very qualities that drive us nuts in the later years (or mere months) of marriage.

How do we accept the other who is different from us? Not by changing the parts that grate, not by glossing over or ignoring them, but by truly and fully embracing the whole person who is your beloved, warts and all.

Marriage is different from other relationships. We all have encounters with people we must tolerate and endure rather than fully accept. Something about them—life-style or personal habits or way of communicating or whatever—drives us nuts.

In a work setting or the like, we have some legitimate options short of full acceptance. Perhaps I can avoid the person or request a transfer or get my boss to impose a solution. Or I can actually confront the problem with that person. But even then, I still have the luxury of dealing with the problem only in the context of getting the job done. It need not invade my entire life (unless, of course, I allow it to do so).

Marriage is different for the simple reason that, to be healthy and good and whole, it must permeate the entire fabric of our lives. It's not a job; it's a vocation calling us beyond avoidance and politeness.

A marriage based on politeness will either explode in rage or be doomed to eternal boredom. Out there in the world, we don't need one hundred percent acceptance of all people in all situations, so we use our social skills to get along. But in marriage, we must move beyond politeness and truly embrace the essential differences between us.

Good Days, OK Days and Bad Days

How do we do this? How do we truly accept the other? I can't say I really know. Every time I think I've got this marriage thing figured out, a new wrinkle appears and throws me off balance. All marriages have their good days, bad days and OK days. The good days are just that—good. The two of us connect on several levels. We live each other's day alongside our own, and it's not hard at all to be friends and lovers. Accepting the other is easy on good days.

The bad days are also just that—bad. We don't connect at all. We irritate each other, and sometimes we say and do things that later require painful forgiveness and reconciliation. On a few bad days, I've wondered if Rene and I are right for each other, if marriage is right for me. Thank God we don't have too many bad days, because accepting the other is basically impossible on those days.

It's the days that are just OK that create the most confusion. You know what I mean: those days when the air is thicker with tension than it ought to be, but neither of you can say just why. The ice is a bit thin and fragile. Do you ever have days when you say "I love you," maybe even several times, but no matter how it is said, it doesn't have quite the desired effect?

The OK days are when I have the hardest time accepting Rene for who she is. But after spending the last seventeen years together, I know (in my head at least) that when I have a problem with Rene, it really is my problem—meaning I also hold the key to its solution. The hardest thing for me to do is look beyond my own self-pity and see the solution. My head knows what I must do, but my heart holds back.

To truly accept Rene for who she is, especially her differences from me, I do better when I look first at myself. In the moment of frustration or battle, when I think Rene is to blame for the problem, I handle it better when I examine myself first. Often I find other irrelevant concerns—job issues, kid problems and such—coloring my feelings and causing more frustration than is warranted. Without this initial check, Rene becomes the victim of problems that aren't hers to begin with.

Then I look at Rene as a whole person. Again, I try to broaden my focus beyond the immediate irritation and put myself in her mind and heart, looking for a rationale. Invariably, when I think the way she does, the logic of her action begins to take shape. More often than not, I find she deserves an apology. Even if that's not the case, we can have a more fruitful conversation about the problem after I've considered her viewpoint.

Then I search for God's grace in the situation. I don't pretend to understand God's logic for the world around me, but the edge of frustration dulls somewhat when I offer a prayer seeking patience and understanding.

This allows me to look at all circumstances of the situation. If I were in her shoes, would I really do any differently or any better? And so what if I would? Under other circumstances, she would clearly outshine me. I'm not Mr. Perfect.

Finally, I simply have to make a choice to accept her for who she is. That choice usually means doing or saying pretty much the opposite of what I feel like saying or doing at the moment. Can I give her a hug instead of a disgusted sigh? Can I offer a compliment instead of a complaint? This does not mean denying my feelings and always being the accommodator. It's more exercising the wisdom of knowing what can be changed and what cannot.

I don't pretend to engage in these five practices all the time but, to repeat, at least my head knows these are the steps to take. On a good day, my heart lines up with my head with no problem. On a bad day—forget it. On OK days I can usually employ two or three of the steps.

I am grateful that Rene and I have mostly good days. We've been graced with the energy and desire to journey with each other, and we are continually enriched by each other's support. But, just as a good day can forge the path for another good day, so too can the OK days perpetuate themselves unless we make a conscious effort to make them otherwise.

Spirituality as Discipline

In their book, *Marrying Well: Stages on the Journey of Christian Marriage,* James and Evelyn Whitehead offer several characteristics of the spirituality of marriage. Interestingly, one of those is discipline. They write, "A spirituality of marriage concerns not only praying together but also developing the skills (or better, the virtues) which make our marriage and family life fruitful. Such a spirituality is, at heart, a discipline." The Whiteheads draw a parallel between Christian life and married life. Both require a sustained commitment and a daily discipline.

I think this is the facet of spirituality called for in fully accepting the other. The virtues of commitment and discipline lead a person into deeper relationship with God, even when the spiritual feelings are absent. When there is no spiritual high, people of faith know that they must persevere in the pursuit of God. This requires discipline. Likewise, when adversity or tragedy strikes, a person may become quite angry with God. Why me? Why this? Why now? But people of faith, even in the midst of anger and frustration, know they must rely on their conviction that God is good and loving.

So, too, with marriage. When it's only an OK day or even a bad day, and the two of us just aren't on the same page together, we must draw on the strength of our long-standing commitment and the discipline of staying present to each other in spite of our desires to be anywhere else at the moment.

Accepting the other requires a spirituality of discipline. Relying solely upon fleeting feelings of warmth, security, comfort and intimacy is doomed. So too, there is great danger in becoming slave to momentary feelings of anger, frustration, even boredom, that are inevitably part of an intimate relationship. Through our lifelong commitment of love and the daily discipline of exercising that commitment, we can find the right perspective for all those feelings—ranging from euphoric joy to intense rage to marked indifference. We don't deny the feelings, but we put them in the context of commitment to each other and our daily efforts to grow in acceptance of the other.

For Reflection and Discussion

- *Would you say you are more married now than on the day of your wedding? How?*

- *Would you say that you have grown in your own personal maturity and self-assurance? How?*

- *Recall and describe a recent event when it was a real challenge for you to pledge your yes to your beloved. How about a recent time when it was easy and joyful?*

- *Are there any long-standing obstacles in the way of your relationship?*

CHAPTER THREE

Upsetting the Balance

R ecall a time in your marriage when the two of you felt
extremely close. You both were cruising on the same
wavelength. Each knew what the other was thinking, feeling
and experiencing. Recall the time when your marriage was as
good as it has ever been. Now, ask yourself how long that
period of intimacy lasted.

As soon as we think we've "arrived" and can coast for
awhile, something surely upsets the balance. The only
constant in a relationship is change. When the two of you
were in that period of closeness, didn't you feel you could
make it last forever? "Let's figure out what we did right, and
just do it over and over again!" Yet the grace of such intense
closeness never lasts because we both continue to grow and
change. Also, there are myriad influences in our lives—work,
children, world events—over which we have no control that
inflict themselves upon the balance of our relationship.

Now, continue your reflection. Only this time recall an
experience when the two of you were completely at odds
with each other. There was seemingly no connection, no
common ground, no light at the end of the tunnel, not even a
desire to understand each other and work through the
problem. How long did that period last?

Again, through change and growth, we move through the
periods of intense struggle in much the same ways that the
periods of joy and intimate closeness always pass. The hurt
may still need reconciling, but intensity of feeling surely
wanes. Often it is better to wait until our feelings cool down
to find forgiveness and reconciliation.

Because we are human, we naturally resist change. Yet,

without change there is no growth. We stagnate and die. Any relationship, especially marriage, requires us to embrace change and growth. Yet, somehow we naturally resist it. Why? Because change upsets our balance. We are caught in limbo between two anchors—the old balance and whatever the new equilibrium will be. Still, amid this anxiety, there is always the opportunity for growth.

Have you noticed how many people would prefer to live with chronic pain—physical, emotional or psychological— than enter into the acute pain that always comes with healing? Even when our balance isn't completely healthy (and it seldom is), we prefer to stay. It's what we're used to. It's familiar and even comfortable. Sure, it may come with some nagging inconvenience or some persistent problem, but at least we know where the land mines and the tender spots are. Why expend all that energy for complete healing? I can live with what I've got.

Yet, we know that the chronic pains of our relationship create a wall of stagnation. Then they fester with anger and hurt that will surely explode in a most untimely manner. As painful as it is, we must embrace the changes of our relationship in order to continue to grow and be ready to experience the next period of deepest intimacy.

Twinings of a Rope

What's the visual image for a couple growing and changing together? Picture the strands of a rope twining themselves around each other. When I was in grade school there was a climbing rope in our gymnasium that was made up of two colored fibers—red and blue.

If the journey of your marriage is like the length of a rope, then the beginning of your rope would certainly look different than your current location on the rope. (I wouldn't venture to say you're at the "end of your rope"!) The different-colored strands affirm that each has his or her own identity, but together we create a whole new identity. Along the rope each strand has been frayed, and perhaps there have been times when your whole marriage was merely hanging on by a thread. Sometimes the strands wrap together well, tightly and securely. Other times they come unraveled, appearing disconnected and exposing vulnerable undersides.

The image of the rope soon breaks down as a metaphor for marriage because it is lifeless and static. A rope is only as strong as its weakest point. Not true for marriage. In fact, the weakest point in a marriage may well reflect its greatest strength. When we overcome serious conflict and reconcile seemingly insurmountable differences, we strengthen the rope of our relationship beyond our imagination.

While the rope is a limited metaphor, allow me to play with the image again. Recalling that two-toned rope from my grade school days, I remember the few times I was able to climb it all the way to the ceiling of the gymnasium. When at the top, I noticed how firmly anchored it was to the ceiling. For the safety of all who climbed, the rope had to be securely anchored there. How securely is our marriage anchored from the top? I know of only one source that can hold us up throughout the duration of our lives together—God. While God cannot keep the rope from becoming tattered and frayed through the changes of our lives, God can keep it securely anchored from above. Any other anchor—money, career, possessions, sometimes even our children—will only hold us down. We need an anchor that holds us up, allowing us to swing through the rhythms and changes of our lives together.

Embracing Change

Choosing change is one thing, but embracing the changes thrust upon us is yet another. Some changes don't enjoy the romantic luster of being "risky"; they are just plain hard. Just when we become comfortable with the status quo, something will undoubtedly upset the balance. Things like illness, pregnancy or the ups and downs of adolescent children have a way of striking at inopportune times.

Or perhaps disillusionment strikes. You know what I mean. Some marriages move from contentment to boredom to downright discontent. And the day comes when the two of you look at each other, both wondering what went wrong. Why do we feel such anger and animosity? Or why do we feel distant and unattached?

These changes demand a response. The temptation to resist, fight or deny the change is great, but to no avail. I met a man who deeply resented that his wife was returning to college after many years of raising children and staying home. While she became invigorated with new ideas, friends and the sheer joy of learning, he became more distant. The more she talked about her classes, the quieter he became. She was torn between the two best things in her life while he was resisting her change and growth with all his might. Fortunately, they realized they needed some help to incorporate her new interests into their marriage. A counselor helped them both identify their feelings surrounding these conflicts and coached them in expressing those feelings.

I have friends whose vision for their marriage is simply to grow old together. They picture themselves in their later years sitting in easy chairs on the front porch. They recognize that the passion of their youth will fade, their strength will diminish and their need for recognition will subside. They simply want to grow old together, and that is enough for them.

With this vision, they are ready to embrace the struggles and changes life throws their way. Why? Because in their hearts, they believe there is an easy chair waiting for them in the end. They cherish the companionship that will come from the memories created now by their years of parenting, working, volunteering and so on.

There is an easy chair waiting: Not a bad vision.

The story of Susan and Bob's twenty-fifth anniversary is appropriate here. Shortly after the Christmas holidays they began discussing how they might celebrate their anniversary the following summer. They knew they wanted to include all their family and friends.

Interestingly, however, Susan and Bob were about to enter the most difficult period of their marriage. Just as many engaged couples begin to struggle and fight and question their commitment just after announcing their engagement, the same phenomenon happened to Bob and Susan as they laid plans for their twenty-fifth anniversary celebration.

Suddenly, everything the other did and said grated. Perhaps it was the pressures of their jobs; both were teachers. Or perhaps it was the pressures of their eight children, four adopted and three "homegrown."

Early in their marriage they had been asked to foster-parent a two-year-old boy who had been removed from his drug-addicted parents. After the allotted months of foster care, Susan and Bob had lost their hearts to the little guy and proceeded to make arrangements to adopt him. Meanwhile, they continued to bear children of their own. Then the agency requested they foster-parent another child. This one had been beaten and abused by her father. The pattern of bonding and falling in love repeated, and she too became a permanent member of the family.

The other two adoptees are brother and sister, and their story, while unique and special, is not unlike the others'. Bob and Susan are clearly gifted with a special charism for welcoming children into their home.

But you can imagine eight children growing up in a home with parents who are schoolteachers. There was a lot of noise, clutter and chaos held together, to be sure, by strong commitment and sincere love. Yet theirs was not a problem-free home. Over the years each child struggled with difficulties. The family made numerous visits to counselors, youth ministers and helping agencies. The family always seemed to be carrying more than its share of emotional crises.

So, perhaps it was simply exhaustion that was tearing at the bond between them. Maybe they were just too tired to carry the baggage, and so they lashed out at each other. As Lent and Easter passed that spring, their marital problems escalated.

Then one evening—one relatively normal evening with the usual family yelling and clutter of dinner dishes—the phone rang. Helen, from the parish hospitality committee, was calling to ask if she and several committee members could come over and talk with Susan and Bob—tonight. Susan stood with the phone to her ear, gazing at the mess, and asked, "Does it have to be tonight?"

Helen responded, "We're considering an important project for the parish and we want to talk with you about it. May we please come over for just a short while?" Against her wishes, Susan agreed. The best they could do on such short notice was simply close off the dining room and kitchen and make a pot of coffee. Then the doorbell rang. The committee members ushered themselves into the living room. Their body language betrayed either nervousness or excitement. When coffee had been served and small talk wound down, Helen came out with her proposal. "The parish has decided to sponsor and host a refugee family, and we have come to ask your advice about adopting new members into the parish family. We can't think of anyone who could give us better advice than you two."

Susan and Bob sat stunned in silence for several moments. Both had been sure they were going to be hit up to volunteer for something. What a nice surprise that all they wanted was advice! But if only Helen and her committee knew the pain and struggles they were having. They wouldn't want the couple's advice if they had seen all that had happened in this house in recent months.

Bob finally broke the silence. Gazing at Susan he said, "Do you remember when we brought Owen home? The scared, frightened look in his eyes? But then remember how over the course of weeks and months that look of fear became one of warmth and love and sparkle? Do you remember that it was his new-found smile that melted us and caused us to fall in love with him?"

Susan nodded, and suddenly all the memories came rushing back. She responded to Bob with another memory of one of their adopted children. Nearly oblivious of Helen and her committee, they talked late into the evening exchanging memories of their adoption stories.

As they talked, you could actually see the healing taking

place. Through stories and memories, Susan and Bob realized all that they had in common, the vast experiences they had shared and the lasting strength of their marriage bond. Their twenty-five years together had been a tremendous journey of change and growth.

In the days and weeks that followed, Susan and Bob could once again see the thread of love and commitment that had woven its way through all the years of their marriage. They were reconnected and ready truly to celebrate their love. Their anniversary celebration that summer was a tremendous success!

Roots and Wings

Perhaps you've heard that the two greatest gifts a parent can give to a child are roots and wings. Roots let children know who they are and where they come from; roots ground them in relationship and family. Wings give them the courage to become the persons God is calling them to be, to pursue their own visions and dreams. Healthy children are gifted with both roots and wings.

These gifts are just as valuable in marriage. After winging away from our families, the two of us put down new roots together that have been growing ever since our wedding day. Together we've developed an identity that is the twining of the strands of our rope. That identity incorporates many facets: habits and beliefs from growing up, our particular personalities, the unique circumstances of our lives coming together, faith and religious practice, friends, surroundings, careers. All these form the roots of our marriage and family.

Our roots also contain the dark side of our relationship: the habits of placating, conflict-avoidance, unfair fighting or any variety of less-than-healthy patterns we may regularly employ. Most couples deal with some issues of power— usually concerning money, sex or time. All couples develop grooves that guide their interaction. Sometimes the grooves become ruts that are nearly impossible to get out of.

Ideally, though, marriage gives us wings as well as roots.

The richness of life created between the two of us is greater than the sum of you plus me. Together we reach well beyond our individual limits with synergistic creative capacity.

What's the clearest, best example of our marriage wings? Our children. The legacy we create through our offspring holds no bounds.

Marital wings also inspire us as individuals. A true best friend and lover brings out the goodness in us that we never knew was there. Imagine what your life would be like if you hadn't married your beloved. I can't speak for you, but I would likely be a rather drab, boring and undermotivated person. In my beloved lies the most concrete and real expression of how God loves life into me. It's no wonder the Scriptures compare the relationship between God and God's people with that of husband and wife. The creativity, love and passion that God has for us is manifested in our own marriage.

I truly admire single people who live a well-rounded, healthy and happy life. I often wonder how they do that on their own. Without the wings of my marriage, I couldn't do it.

Through the Years

Take a reflective moment to go back in time and see how your relationship has evolved over the years. To do this you will need to find your wedding picture. With luck, you won't have to rummage around too long in the attic to find one.

Study yourself in the picture. Look beyond the outdated styles of clothing and hair and allow the image to bring back memories of your life then. What were your personal hopes, dreams, struggles and conflicts? What were the key factors in your life then?

Now go to the mirror. Take a good hard look at your face and ask yourself the same questions. What are your hopes and dreams now? You are the same person, of course, but you've also changed. Life has weathered you and, I hope, instilled wisdom.

Go back to the wedding picture. This time, study the one

you married. Recall his or her hopes, dreams and ambitions, which, surely, the two of you shared. Now go to your beloved. Study his or her face. What do you know about his or her current dreams, goals and ambitions? How has he or she changed and evolved?

Finally, look at the two of you together in the picture. Study yourselves as a couple. What was your vision for the new family you created on your wedding day? Now think through the years of your marriage. What have been the highlights, the low points, the challenges that you have negotiated well together? What would you have done differently had you better understood what the other was going through?

Bring the time line up to the present. Mentally look at the two of you together. Is there any resemblance to the wedding picture of years ago? What keeps you together? What is the common thread that weaves its way through your lives?

How would you articulate a spirituality of change? Several ideas come to my mind. One notion is that prayer and faith are what keep the two of us together as we navigate the rough waters of change. Spirituality provides the anchor that we can always trust; something secure, real and safe. When all else is unsure and unpredictable, we can always come back to our spiritual roots.

This posture helps a couple find balance and a measure of peace amid their frenetic lives. When the pace of life accelerates, there is all the more reason to take enough time, both individually and as a couple, to bring ourselves to a quiet stop and allow God to speak into our silence. Yet, if you're like us, the hardest times to stop and pray are the very times we need it most. The busier my life gets, the more I become a human doing rather than a human being. And I haven't figured out how to pray unless I'm in a state of "being."

This posture is challenging, yes, but we try to hold each other accountable. Through gentle reminders and invitations, we encourage each other to stay in touch with (or get back in touch with) the persistent presence of the Spirit.

Another take on the spirituality of change is to rely on faith and belief as a guide to right choice and decisionmaking. When our family moved across town several years ago, we were confronted with the decision of school choice for our sons. It seemed straightforward and logical to me: Send them to the neighborhood school. Yet Rene was not so sure. She suggested we pray about it.

I didn't think that was necessary because my mind was made up and I didn't want anything (least of all God) to mess up my plans. But how do you decline an invitation to pray with your spouse? As you might imagine, our discernment led to a different choice of schools—which, as you might also imagine, quickly proved to be the better choice.

Afterwards I realized that my "logical conclusion" was flawed by selfishness. I considered the neighborhood school the best choice primarily because the boys could walk to it, which meant that I would no longer have to do the morning school run. Sometimes prayer and discernment can reveal a hidden personal agenda that isn't always healthy.

Similarly, prayer and faith can empower a couple to make a difficult, but necessary choice. When confronted with change, one or both spouses may be resistant. As I mentioned, most of us prefer to live with chronic pain rather than endure the acute pain of healing. Yet spiritual exercising may rightfully challenge both to put out the extra energy and endure the struggle that accompanies transition from one state to the next.

Faith may be our only friend in the face of unpleasant choices. What parent hasn't heard from a child at the top of his or her lungs, "I hate you!" only to hope and pray that someday the child will be grateful for the hard stand that was taken? Similarly, what spouse has not been confronted with the hard truth from the loved one about something said or unsaid, about something done or left undone? Knowing that my spouse is a person of genuine faith challenges me to hear her through my own faith, and it assures me that she tells me the hard truth out of sincere and lasting love. Faith is a friend we can count on.

As lifetime partners, we can tap into a spiritual energy that surrounds the moments of uncertainty and change. With change come risk and vulnerability—that experience of being exposed to the elements and having little or no control over the outcome. Yet, as a couple, we occasionally have the courage to join the presence of the Spirit in the uncertainty itself.

This is the essence of marriage, is it not? On your wedding day you laid your very life into the hands of another person without knowing what the future held. Yet it didn't take long to discover the risk and vulnerability involved in your choice.

As idealism fades into realism, the choice to risk and be vulnerable becomes all the more reflective of a true covenant of love. It's one thing to give my life over to my ideal image of Rene, but it takes superhuman courage to offer myself when I know her in full reality. In short, it takes more faith to stay married than it does to get married.

This kind of love, I contend, is not humanly possible. By that, I mean, the two of us cannot keep it up all on our own. While each day presents a call to recommit ourselves, there have surely been occasions that call for a bigger yes, for relinquishing more control than we thought possible, for revealing more vulnerability than ever before. These moments require more faith than we thought we had. These challenges always come in the midst of highly stressful, difficult times when one or both of us are already weak and distracted.

These are the times when God is the only one to trust. Neither of us has enough strength, patience, courage or simple presence to sustain each other. But the mystery of the Spirit can find a way through the darkness, if we abandon ourselves to it—as difficult and illogical as that is.

Few things are as complicated and taxing as intimacy sustained with one person over time. Sooner or later we reach a point where we're both hanging on by a thread. This is the spirituality of change: when it's clear that the other cannot give the support I need, cannot hold me up, but I lay my life in her hands anyway. In doing so, I lay my life in the Lord's hands.

For Reflection and Discussion

- *How have the two of you intertwined your changes in creating the rope that is your marriage? When have you been frayed while the other held strong, and vice versa? Have your twinings ever come unraveled? Have you ever been hanging on by a mere thread?*

- *Threads that can weave their way through your marriage are prayer and spirituality. How have the two of you acknowledged and incorporated God into your lives? How do you recognize the subtle movement of the Spirit in your relationship? How do you express your beliefs in that which is real but unseen?*

PART TWO

The Arenas of Marriage Spirituality

Relying on the "four postures" of a healthy marriage (Part One) as a foundation, the remainder of this book will explore seven specific arenas of married life where spirituality can flourish, where God can be found in the ordinary, where the mysterious meshes with the mundane—all to provide a leaven for a truly rich and, dare I say, holy life.

Let me first share with you an insight that has helped me a great deal. Very simply, the insight is recognizing and understanding the difference between God's transcendent love and God's immanent love.

Many of us have a better understanding of God's transcendent love. This refers to the idea that God is so great, so awesome, so magnificent that God is literally "out of this world." That's just what *transcendent* means. God far exceeds any human effort at full understanding. Knowing we cannot fully embrace all that is God, how do we go about trying to do so in our spiritual journey? Well, if the God we seek transcends our immediate world, wouldn't it make sense to try to do the same? This is the core of monastic spirituality: Remove ourselves from the noise, clutter and distractions of life, and we can more easily and more richly connect with the transcendent God.

This is why we seek solitude, quiet and peace when we go to pray. This is why we go on retreat. God's transcendent love is found when we empty our minds and hearts of all the noise and distractions of life. When we spend time in quiet prayer and meditation, we ground ourselves with the real but unseen God and we are strengthened to face the pressures of our day.

God's immanent love isn't exactly the opposite of transcendence, but it is a complement. While God is literally "out of this world," God is at the same time as close as the air we breathe. The breadth and depth of God's love is so great we can find it *within* the noise and clutter and sometimes chaos of our lives.

God's immanent love opens up the possibility of a spirituality that complements the monastic style of solitude, meditation and contemplation. It is a spirituality of movement and noise. It is the art of discovering the Spirit within those very things that some would consider distractions.

Ideally, one's spirituality includes the pursuit of both the immanent and the transcendent God. One is not better than the other. I take great comfort in this distinction. Why? Because my life-style does not lend itself to frequent and prolonged periods of solitude and prayerful meditation. Sitting down to pray in a corner of our house mysteriously sends a signal to all family members that now is the exact time they need to ask Dad a question or dust that very corner or vacuum that room. So, while my efforts to await God's love in stillness are often thwarted, I am grateful for God's presence in the here and now.

Yet the pursuit of God's transcendent love is not just for the monks, mystics and monastics. We all need regular periods of quiet and solitude amid the frenetic pace of life. If I don't take a few minutes for quiet centering each morning, I literally don't make it to the end of the day. I lose my ability to be present to others, even to myself, long before I am allowed to seek my bed again. Yet the essence of spirituality, as I've said before, is presence. If I can't be present to myself or others, I certainly cannot tune into the presence of the Spirit.

While we have been developing monastic spirituality for centuries, development of a spirituality of immanence has been far less systematic. Therefore, folks like you and me must take the risk to share the simple encounters with God that occur in our daily lives to enrich and enliven this spirituality.

God's immanent love is rooted in the very nature of married and household life, that is, in intimate relationship. Instead of trying to adapt a monastic-style spirituality to the hectic lives we lead as spouses, parents and workers, we seek to develop a spirituality that emerges from the very essence of our lives "in the world."

The following chapters explore seven arenas of married life where the spirituality of immanence can be nurtured: intimacy; partnership; conflict; health; parenting; work, career and vocation; and play.

For Reflection and Discussion

- *How do you experience the transcendence of God's love? How and where do you see the awesomeness, the otherworldliness of God?*

- *How about God's immanent love? When do you experience God in the "creases and folds" of your daily life?*

- *How do you discover these in your beloved?*

CHAPTER FOUR

The Spirituality of Intimacy

"There is something whimsical about a God who invented the giraffe, and the rhino and the hairy-nosed wombat. Not to mention sex." (William J. O'Malley, S.J., in *The People's Catechism*)

Someone once said that the secret of life is not that we should love God, but that God loves us. All love and desire originate from God. But because we are merely human, we can only experience love through our human filter. This is not all bad. I, for one, greatly enjoy the fact that I experience love and pleasure via the human body: my own and my beloved's. If we weren't human, there'd be no embodied love.

In our humanness, we express, though imperfectly, God's idea of love. Father John Heagle, noted author and lecturer on relationships and sexuality, said it well in a presentation to the 1995 Call to Action Conference in Chicago:

> This is the quiet story of longing, yearning and restlessness in our souls, our immense desire for happiness.... God is the primal seeker; the original pursuer of hearts. God put the yearning for love in us, so that one day we might discover that we have already been loved from the beginning. God put restlessness in us so that we might find our rest and aliveness in loving.

More than any other virtue, love is the one God wants us to practice. We can only love as humans, embodied with desires, urges, passions and drives. Without these, love would be impossible. Without love, we cannot be creatures in God's

43

image. And so we journey through life seeking relationship and intimacy.

Being completely naked and vulnerable before my best friend and then fully embraced with genuine love and passion has got to be like meeting God face-to-face. It's no wonder the Bible uses the love of husband and wife to attempt to describe God's love for all people. It is a love filled with passion, desire and delight. It is a love that is pure and good. It is a love that delights in body and sensuality.

The Song of Songs portrays two lovers expressing their sensual delight in each other. Read a passage or two from it. Its descriptions are explicit, sexual and passionate. The two lovers clearly rejoice in each other's bodies, hearts and souls without reservation or apology.

> How beautiful you are, my love,
>   how very beautiful!
> Your eyes are doves....
> Your lips are like a crimson thread,
>   and your mouth is lovely.
> Your cheeks are like halves of a pomegranate....
> Your two breasts are like two fawns,
>   twins of a gazelle,
>   that feed among the lilies.... (Song 4:1a, 3, 5)
>
> I am my beloved's
>   and his desire is for me.
> Come, my beloved,
>   let us go forth into the fields....
> There I will give you my love. (Song 7:10-11a, 12c)

Can you believe this is in the Bible? Perhaps God's love is not much different from the best of human love.

Intimacy

Intimacy is the day-to-day expression and experience of my relationships. It is more than just being close and sharing loving feelings. Whenever a relationship manifests itself in any form, intimacy is created. So I experience intimacy when I just think of Rene, when we visit on the phone, take a walk, fight with each other, reconcile, console each other, parent our children and, certainly, when we make love.

God is our model for expressing love and exploring intimacy. As we embrace the beloved, the love of God comes back to us in a profound and unique way. We don't just model God's unconditional love in marriage, we actually experience it. We don't just model God's idea of intimacy in sexual lovemaking, we experience it. This is what is meant by incarnation: God actually entering into the human condition, embracing the totality of being a person.

In their book, *The Soul of a Marriage*, Patrick J. and Claudette M. McDonald say:

> Because God entered into the mainstream of life in this fashion, all reality, every interaction of the human endeavor is embraced by this loving God and is therefore sacred. The awareness of this reality of the incarnation...offers the couple a grounding in the very life of God. Through every action of love, they make the presence of God more real.

Intimacy is much bigger and broader than sexual lovemaking. We experience intimacy in parenting, running and maintaining our home, sharing the joys and woes of our work, being best friends, reading, studying and learning together, worshiping and praying together, dealing with misfortune and stress, and so on. Intimacy names what the two of us experience together as we maneuver our lives through time.

Intimacy, like spirituality, is a reflection of presence. It is an expression that offers myself to you at this moment with no strings, completely vulnerable, as you do the same. I trust that you will cherish and nurture me, and I will do the same for you. And God is present here in dynamic ways because God also yearns for relationship and intimacy. The McDonalds say it well: "God is lover, who wants union with the beloved. In marital spirituality, the passion of the Beloved is mediated and concretized through the love of husband and wife for one another."

There is, then, no richer expression of intimacy than sexual lovemaking. I stand before Rene truly naked and vulnerable and invite her to do the same. Yet I stand there with strong desires, not just for her, for her body, but more so for the rich and luxurious closeness I know we can experience together when we offer each other ultimate presence: physical, emotional, intellectual and certainly spiritual.

And when we wash ourselves in the ultimate presence of each other, the intimacy lingers long after the lovemaking is over, permeating the other arenas of our lives that beforehand seemed so much less than stellar.

While our sexual sharing is just one of many intimate arenas, it is perhaps the most powerful. As you know, the arenas of marriage are not mutually exclusive. The quality and depth of intimacy experienced in one will influence that of another. This is perhaps most true for sexual intimacy. We don't make love well when we've been fighting over finances or struggling over the family calendar. We don't make love well when one of us is ill and therefore cannot be as present to the other.

Sacred Sexual Intimacy

Many couples experience spiritual growth through sexual intimacy—and not by accident or happenstance. They seek a spiritual dimension to their lovemaking, leading them to a deeper awareness of God in their lives.

What is holy and sacred about sex? When I asked several couples this question, their responses were straightforward and insightful. There was little hesitancy, and their responses had more clarity than I would have guessed.

One woman said that she often feels transported to another place that is literally out of this world.

> Sometimes when we make love, I lose touch with everything around me and feel as though I'm in a distant land. It's lovely, safe and has no boundaries. I sometimes wonder if that isn't what heaven is like.

It's easy to imagine meeting God there. It's the kind of place where God would be found.

So I guess I would say that our lovemaking is sacred because it sometimes puts me in a "space" where I know God is also present. I'm not talking about the physical pleasure and sensation, although that's very real and wonderful. Occasionally our lovemaking is a rich, pure spiritual experience for me, and then I know God is real because as I become one with my husband, I also feel fused with God.

A husband responded by saying:

Together we create something much bigger than ourselves, and sometimes we just lie there in awe of what we have experienced. During those times, it's easier to understand God's awesome love. When I feel so filled with love, I feel powerful and god-like in the best sense.

One woman married twenty years commented:

We've always counted on God being with us in our marriage, especially when we have sex. Sometimes we say a prayer beforehand, sometimes not. But either way, we know that it's not just the two of us there in the bedroom.

A husband said:

Sex is holy and sacred because it, more than any other part of our marriage, represents the Sacrament of Marriage. I was taught that a sacrament is a visible expression of the invisible God, or something like that. Well, there is no more concrete expression of pure love that I've ever known than when we make love together. I was also taught that God is love. Through Lisa, I've known genuine love, so I think I can say I have also encountered God.

Another woman's comments were very honest and touching. Just as we encounter dry and dark periods along our spiritual journey, so too with sexual intimacy.

Our lovemaking isn't always great. In fact, we've gone through periods when it has been rather difficult and unsatisfying. This has caused anger and misunderstanding between us because sex is important to us both. We've done a lot of talking and praying about it.

Yet even in the midst of the hard times we've always approached our lovemaking with a sense of reverence and awe. It's like we both know there's more to sex than what the two of us bring to it. There's something mysterious and spiritual about it that is both lovely and elusive at the same time. Perhaps that's what makes it holy and sacred. If it wasn't an elusive mystery, and was always completely available to us, would we be able to fully appreciate its value and power?

These comments led me to ask how a couple's sexual intimacy can foster their spirituality as a couple. Again, the comments were clear and practical. "Experiencing God in our lovemaking helps me find God in the other areas of our marriage too," said one husband.

Another husband commented:

When we make love, we surrender ourselves completely to each other. It has taken me a long time to learn to surrender. I'm a person who needs to be in control at all times, and this was a problem for us early in our marriage. My need for control meant that we were always in a power struggle with each other, and sex was a potent weapon that I used in subtle ways. But through Joan's patience, a lot of talking and more than a few tears from both of us, I'm learning to relinquish control and surrender myself to Joan. I'm also learning to surrender myself to God.

Several comments centered around the need to maintain regular contact with each other in marriage, and with God through prayer and spirituality.

When we don't make love for a long time, we lose

touch with each other, and it's harder to reconnect. The same is true with God. If we lose touch, it's harder to find the Spirit again.

Of course, obstacles arise to prevent couples from sexual intimacy: illness, travel separation, pregnancy, to name a few. Yet these couples emphasized the need to stay in touch with each other in any way possible, if only by letter and telephone—and, when possible, to offer a lot of touch to each other. "If sex is not possible, offer caressing, massage, holding—anything physical." Touch like this, they added, is just as important when sex is available.

One couple offered a fascinating insight. They understood traditional spirituality as drawing a clear and hard distinction between sacred and profane, spirit and flesh. However, they insisted that when they experience the ultimate of flesh and body with each other, it literally opens the floodgates to the realm of the spirit. Their sexual sharing becomes a genuine union of body and spirit. They conclude, quite accurately, that their lovemaking is their best expression of prayer.

Again, Father John Heagle has a nice insight:

> It's no accident, is it, that the language of mysticism and the poetry of human passion are the same. Both speak of yearning, seeking, the pain of absence, the joy of finding, the fire and the ecstasy of union. I only want to remind you of something you already know deep down inside. Sexuality and spirituality are not only not enemies, they are friends. They are companions on the journey.

These couples maintain that sexual intimacy is a source of inspiration and motivation to pursue a spiritual encounter. Quite simply, they find God in their lovemaking. They also feel as though they can stay in touch with God beyond the immediate intimate encounter. The spirituality of the event lingers and permeates the rhythms of their lives. Their sexual sharing bridges the transcendent world and the here-and-now. This is, of course, exactly what the mystics have searched for down through the ages.

Love is the source of relationship. Relationship is the source of intimacy. In the image and likeness of God, humans are lovable and capable of love. In the image and likeness of God, humans seek relationship and intimacy—an inherent human need. In the image and likeness of God, humans create life and love. For "God is love and those who abide in love abide in God, and God abides in them" (1 John 4:16b).

For Reflection and Discussion

- *What is your sense of the intimacy you share with your spouse? What feelings or thoughts do you find it easiest to share deeply? Are there times when it is difficult to be open? Are there times when you are reluctant to be close?*

- *How has your lovemaking changed over the years of your marriage?*

- *What do you find holy and sacred about your sexual intimacy?*

- *Complete these statements: "When we make love, I really appreciate ____." "When we make love, I need ____."*

CHAPTER FIVE

The Spirituality of Partnership

Charlie and Janna are both self-employed, working out of their home. They've been married fourteen years and have three children, the oldest on the verge of adolescence. The younger two are still elementary-school age. Janna works part-time as a bookkeeper for small businesses. She tries to keep her working hours confined to the kids' school hours. During summer months, it's a bit of a juggling act between the kids' needs and her clients', but she makes it work.

Charlie just recently left his salaried position with a company to try to make a go of it as an independent consultant. Laughingly, he comments, "Yeah, I must be a fool to leave a fully furnished, air-conditioned office complete with secretarial pool for a cramped work space in a makeshift closet-type room (with just a small window) in the basement of our home. When I'm not on the road, I'll be living, eating, sleeping and working at home."

This arrangement wouldn't suit most families, but Janna and Charlie are confident they can do it. Charlie comments, "I have no illusions that our jobs won't challenge our partnership as a couple. But we've discovered a few skills and patterns to help us juggle our jobs, marriage and family all under one roof. It's a challenge, to be sure, and some days are better than others, but on the whole it seems to be working."

Some of the partnership skills that Charlie refers to include:

- Recognizing that the work or current responsibility of one of them is not inherently more important than that of the other. While some tasks may rate a higher priority than others, this does not mean one spouse is more important.

- Realizing that the more they talk about and inform each other of the little, day-to-day concerns, the easier it is to strategize around the big issues that arise.

- Remembering that each segment of life (job, marriage, children, home) deserves its own time, space, energy and attention. While these varied arenas are linked, they must maintain some distinct identity.

- Maintaining a balance between giving each other needed personal time and holding each other accountable for his or her contribution to the marriage and family.

- Deliberately creating a working partnership, talking about it often and making the best use of each other's strengths while complementing each other's areas of weakness.

Charlie and Janna will surely put these skills to the test in the coming months and years. One skill that can be added to Charlie's list is maintaining realistic expectations.

Realistic Expectations

If our expectations of each other and our marriage are not well grounded, then our partnership is in trouble. In their book, *Promises to Keep: Developing the Skills of Marriage*, Thomas H. Hart and Kathleen Fischer cite four false expectations that many carry into marriage and some take years to unlearn. (See "Keeping Expectations Reasonable," pages 71-77.) From these false assumptions I would like to offer four realistic expectations that form a solid foundation for a lively, enjoyable and effective partnership between husband and wife.

1) *False Assumption:* "I expect my mate to meet all my needs." I'll wager most us entered marriage with some notion of "living happily ever after," meaning we'll never

want for anything that our spouse cannot do for us. After all, that's exactly what we've been groomed to expect from marriage. A part of me expects Rene to satisfy all my needs, as well as most of my wants. While I know this isn't realistic or possible, the feeling lingers.

Of course we have different interests, likes and dislikes. Yet I hang onto a dream of always doing everything together—working, playing, loving, parenting—and enjoying every minute of it. Funny, though, in my dream we only do the things I love and enjoy, many of which (in real life) are not the least bit interesting or desirable to Rene. And, of course, many activities in her dream I would find quite tedious.

Revised Assumption: I must meet some of my needs on my own in order to bring balance and vitality to my marriage. While she is certainly my best friend, Rene cannot be my only friend. While her world is rich and full of stimulation and learning, I need a broader world than just hers.

When I bring to Rene the richness of learning I've experienced in, say, a class or a trip, it becomes a new little arena for us to share intimacy. When I share with her the enjoyment of making a new friend or going to a deeper level of friendship with someone I've known for a while, that too becomes a source of enjoyment and vitality in our marriage. We find the synergy when we bring our experiences to each other and share their richness.

We would likely not stay married if we existed only in each other's worlds. We constantly need fresh input from those around us to liven our souls and check our egos. As attractive as it may sound on the surface, an isolated tropical island existence for the rest of our lives would likely be a disaster.

2) *False Assumption:* "The state of marriage will bring me fulfillment and complete contentment." Another fairy-tale notion that many of us were steeped in is the expectation that simply being married will fulfill all our needs and wants, and that it will be a perfect fit for our life-style. I have been destined for marriage since I was born, and

have now finally arrived, which means I no longer need to be concerned about it.

Revised Assumption: Marriage is a partnership we create together, not a "state" that we enter, subjecting ourselves to its influence. Our partnership is active, not passive. It is built on love, commitment, passion and mutuality. And only through this active partnership do we each acquire the true identity of spouse.

Marriage shapes my core identity. It affects my entire life and all my relationships. But it does not usurp my entire identity. I am not allowed to hide behind the label "married man," as if that gives me permission to forsake individual, personal responsibilities.

Each marriage is a unique partnership that can never be replicated. Our partnership is comprised of the unique personalities and experiences each of us brings to the marriage. Our partnership has some strengths that are perhaps unsurpassed by any other couple in history, and it also has some needs and weaknesses that are uniquely our own. Marriage is not simply a social state of being.

3) *False Assumption:* "We know we'll have occasional problems and spats, but ours is a 'good marriage,' so we won't have to deal with serious problems. We are so compatible, and we've built such a strong, loving relationship in all areas that we're simply destined to spend the rest of our days in loving bliss together."

You don't even have to finish reading these sentences to see their folly. Yet, how many us went to the altar with this expectation? Of course, we have a lot in common; there's something about us that "clicks." We have a deep rapport that can (and has) carried us through some hard times. If our relationship didn't have these characteristics, we wouldn't have married in the first place.

Yet, as we will see in the next chapter, these characteristics in no way prevent us from encountering serious conflict at one time or another. These times of darkness may be related to a job loss or even a promotion, chronic illness or serious injury, a crisis of addiction, an affair, the loss of a child, depression or to discovering more of one's self and needing to make changes. Some of these hard times may be so difficult we may consider ending the marriage. No matter how compatible, all couples are susceptible to serious conflict.

Revised Assumption: A true partnership in marriage grows and develops in spite of serious dark times—even as a result of those struggles. Our love is not static, but grows deeper and stronger with experiences of struggle. We may have established some healthy or not-so-healthy partnership patterns early on, but these will certainly be refined, adjusted, deepened or even changed altogether as the years go on. We can also develop new partnership skills specifically by weathering the dark times of our marriage.

4) *False Assumption:* "As my best friend, my beloved will always be on my side. Even when all others have let me down or when life is lonely and no other friends remain, I know my beloved will always side with me and bring me the comfort I need." This is one of those assumptions that has some credibility, but still is not true.

A true best friend remains loyal and loving, especially during difficult, lonely times. But he or she also remains true to covenant love, which means challenging the other to see his or her blind spots or shortcomings, even allowing the other to endure the darkness for the sake of growth.

Over a lifetime, friendship has its ups and downs. In some periods, whether brief or prolonged, our friendship is strained and difficult. At other times, of course, we are rock solid with each other. But the covenant nature of marriage allows our love to endure.

Revised Assumption: Regardless of the current status of our friendship, we are "Number One" for each other in our exclusive intimate relationship. We may not do together what best friends do, and some of our interests may clash. (She loves to dance; he has two left feet. He has a passion for golf; she'll never understand why people chase that little white ball.) But the arenas of intimacy we share encompass far more than just the activities that friends share. We have built a life, a family, a real home together, all founded on love, passion, commitment and partnership. We have formed a bond that goes deeper and carries more meaning than friendship, and our commitment to each other surpasses any other friendship either of us may have.

Our faith and our intention to find God's love in our relationship buoy us up when friendship lets us down. The sacramental nature of our covenant bridges the gaps of our human shortcomings. Even when we haven't been very good friends with each other, we know there is something bigger than the two of us wrapping us in love and commitment.

The Spirituality of Partnership

Where is God in the partnership of marriage? Perhaps the most concrete daily expressions of partnership lie in the Sacrament of Marriage. In living our partnership, we also model God's covenant of love with all humankind.

At some point in your life you probably heard the definition of a sacrament as "an outward sign of an inward grace." This definition is still quite valid. The outward sign of Baptism, for example, is the water in which the child or adult is immersed, symbolizing the cleansing grace of new life in Christ. While immersion into water is the outward sign, the internal grace of Baptism is expressed throughout the child's faith life with support and encouragement from parents, godparents and the believing community.

The sacramental symbolism of marriage is also very rich. Two people come together in love and commitment. They pledge to remain together in sickness and in health, in good times and bad, until death. Theirs is a covenant of love rooted in trust and commitment. Yet the Christian community believes there is still more to this covenant than the personal promise of two lovers. Their personal, human pledge also symbolizes God's unconditional love for all people and

Christ's love for the Church. The outward sign of two people pledging their lives to each other reflects the inward grace of God's unbreakable covenant with the human race.

During the wedding, it is not the priest who confers Matrimony (as he does the other sacraments), but the couple themselves. The priest is merely the official witness of the believing community. But remember the adage, "A wedding lasts for a day, while a marriage lasts a lifetime." The full expression of the sacrament comes only through the day-to-day faithful expression of the covenant celebrated on the wedding day.

When we use our partnership skills in marriage we not only nurture our friendship and love, we also symbolize and reveal God's active love for all people. As Christian believers, our covenant of love is much more than just a personal promise between us. It is a model of lasting love for all believers. And it is in our partnership that this is best expressed everyday.

In his book, *Marriage and Sacrament: A Theology of Christian Marriage*, Michael G. Lawler describes the covenant of marriage. He also alludes to the notion of sacramental partnership.

> To covenant is to consent and to commit oneself radically and solemnly....[The partners] commit themselves mutually to create and to sustain a climate of personal openness, availability and trust. They commit themselves mutually to rules of behavior which will respect, nurture and sustain intimate communion and steadfast love. They commit themselves mutually to explore together the religious depth of human life in general, and of their marriage in particular, and to respond to that depth in the light of their shared Christian faith. They commit themselves mutually to abide in love, in covenant, in marriage and in sacrament for the whole of life. They commit themselves to create a life of equal and intimate partnership in loyal and faithful love.

Janna and Charlie, whose story began this chapter, face a

unique challenge since both are self-employed, working out of their home. They will need fully to employ all those partnership skills Charlie named (see page 51). But that will not be enough. They will not succeed all by themselves, regardless of how well versed they are in communication, listening and conflict-resolution. They must root their love in covenant and sacrament. They must trust in the mysteries of sacramental love to carry them when mere skills come up short and their friendship is strained.

When the believing couple lives out their partnership together, they express the richness of their sacramental covenant. They also enrich their marriage spirituality.

For Reflection and Discussion

- *What are one or two false assumptions you carried into your marriage? What would be the revised assumptions?*

- *What does the word* partnership *mean to you? How would you describe the unique strengths and weaknesses of your marriage partnership?*

- *What are the most important partnership skills the two of you use regularly? What skills could use some improvement?*

- *How would you describe the "friendship" the two of you share? When your friendship is strained, how do you feel, and what do you do about it?*

CHAPTER SIX

Spirituality and Conflict

The Dark Night

The night descends upon me.
I fall into an underground cavern.
The place they call darkness
is the crucible of my purification.

The darkness erupts
from a thousand fires of emptiness within
and moves to consume me.
Dark ashes scatter over the earth.

When will this pain stop?
My being trembles as
the pain intensifies to a
deep unquenchable inferno.

Where are you, my God?
Lift me out of the blazing fire
and soothe me with the cooling breezes
    of your love.
(Patrick and Claudette McDonald,
    The Soul of a Marriage)

The flip side of the coin of intimacy is conflict. To sustain
closeness with another, one must expect struggle and strife.
Conflict is just as inherent in human relationships as intimacy
and love. We don't seek it, of course, but it plays an important
cleansing role in the marriage relationship.

Because conflict is innate in human relationship, God is
also present in our struggles. The Spirit lingers in and around
our pain and anger, inviting both of us to grow beyond our
unrealistic expectations and shortsightedness. The Spirit does

not reduce the pain, for therein lies the purification that leads to healing. But somehow God offers courage to bear the pain and see our way through to healing.

Lori describes her marriage struggles:

> My need for more space and independence had been growing steadily for at least the last four years. I always assumed that when the kids got a little older and more self-sufficient I'd have more time to myself, a little more freedom.
>
> But that hasn't happened. The kids are teens now and they sure require more time than I had anticipated. Everyone just assumes that I will take care of everything: running them to games, dances and wherever, fixing all the meals and keeping the whole house running smoothly.
>
> Andy is like having a fourth child around here, expecting dinner on the table every night and a steady supply of clean underwear. I've always had to take full responsibility for our relationship. If he ever wants to be close and loving, he doesn't show it anymore—just waits for me to take the initiative. If we want to go out, I have to dream up the ideas, make all the arrangements, and then drag him along while he complains that we should have chosen a movie instead.
>
> I know this doesn't make sense, but I need more independence from Andy and the kids, and at the same time I need more love and intimacy. I just want him to show some spark of interest in me, purely for my sake, to see the real me. And I crave the time and space to further develop my own interests.
>
> He seldom touches me anymore. You know, the simple touch of friendship—laying his hand on mine during conversation, a brief shoulder rub, even a pesky pat on the rear. I feel I've become just a source for clean shirts and a hot meal at the end of his busy day.
>
> I know it's partly my fault, because earlier in our marriage, I actually liked the supportive role, where the wife does all she can to help her man succeed out

there in the tough and dangerous world. I liked keeping house and raising babies. I prided myself on doing it well, and we were nearly always ready and waiting when Daddy walked through the door. So I can see how I helped create the pattern.

But I cannot deny what's happening in me now. I need more in my life than just playing housekeeper for these four people I live with. I'm ready to fulfill a dream or two of my own, and that's going to mean somebody else has to pick up the slack around here.

It was the hardest thing I've ever done to tell him these things. I knew he wouldn't understand, and I also knew he'd be hurt and angry. I didn't want to tell him that night. I mean I hadn't planned it. But the kids were out and the house was so quiet I found myself feeling depressed. He asked me what was wrong. I just said "nothing," hoping he would leave me alone. But he kept pressing me and asking what was bugging me, and so after a while I basically exploded.

For the next hour I just spouted off with my feelings, complaints, hurts and memories of all the times when I've felt this way. Once the floodgates opened, I couldn't shut them off. I knew I was hurting him, but I couldn't help it. I had to get it all out.

When I finally stopped, he just sat there in silence. He was stunned and his eyes were glazed. After a long silence, he started slowly to shake his head. We were in the living room and I was sitting on the couch and he was in the easy chair. He was just shaking his head, and it seemed he wanted to say something, but no sound came out. Finally, he just got up and walked out of the room.

I was devastated. I had just poured out my heart and soul to him, risked all that we had by laying it on the table, and he didn't have one word of response. He just drove another nail in the coffin of my heart with that move. It would've been better had he blown up in anger, but the silent treatment is the worst. Men are so—I don't know.

Lori never felt more alone in her life. Her reward for speaking the truth, laying out her feelings, finally being completely vulnerable and claiming her own needs was abandonment. Andy walked out, leaving everything up in the air—including Lori's bleeding heart. Lori also wondered where God was in this hour of need.

Meanwhile, Andy felt blindsided. He had no idea such a storm was brewing. He was caught completely unaware; both mind and heart locked up on him. "I just had to get out of there," he muses. "Where did this outburst come from? What had I done to deserve this? She really went off the deep end."

Conflict is inevitable in marriage, and everybody knows that. But when it strikes with such force as it did with Lori and Andy, knowing this fact does nothing to lessen the pain. It's normal, really, for a spouse to reach a point in the relationship where she or he needs more space and independence. Those internal questions of the heart that go to the core of one's identity can overflow into consciousness and simply must be addressed. Yet in marriage, anger and resentment typically accompany the outpouring of these questions. It's not possible to remain calm and rational when confronted with such core life-concerns. And when it seems your beloved has prevented you from pursuing your dreams and needs for years or even decades, resentment is unavoidable.

In the effort to realign independence and togetherness, all the fantasies of marriage begin to explode. One wonders just who one married. The gap between image and reality is stark and deep. Spouses find themselves wondering how they could have been so close just days ago and now find such a chasm between them. Andy wondered if he and Lori had been living the same marriage. She seemingly placed the entire blame for her anger and unhappiness squarely on him, painting him dark and sinister so as to give her the excuse she needed to break out and find her independence.

While not every marital conflict is so deep, most couples encounter a darkness such as this at some time. Even though the crisis is often a result of one person's growth and development, the pain and anguish for both are severe and, sadly, many couples do not emerge from the darkness still together. Yet most find a way through to daylight again. Grace is available; while it does nothing to reduce the pain, it offers an added measure of courage and perseverance—usually just enough.

Spirituality for the couple in darkness is hard to find and even harder to express and share with each other. Yet God is accessible in dark times, amid the pain, anger and frustration.

Conflict usually leads to individual retreat, either to avoid battle or to tend wounds. This inward focus leads to spiritual questions: God, where are you? Is this person really the one I married? Am I the cause of the problem? Am I the one changing? Why? Why must everything look so hopeless?

Surrender

But each must first surrender—to self, to the other, to the realities of their relationship and ultimately to God. The concept of surrender is rich and full, as Patrick J. and Claudette M. McDonald describe in their book *The Soul of a Marriage*:

> Surrender does not mean an abandonment of all hopes of reclaiming a faltering marriage.... Surrender implies something inherently more healing: to surrender to the realization that the marriage must undergo profound changes if it is to survive. The shadows of control, resentment, manipulation and inflexible patterns of behavior must go. Revitalization of the marriage demands a deeper self-evaluation than a spouse ever imagined.

The process of surrender makes more room for God to dwell in the hearts of the couple. We're talking about mature love here. When simple romance has been diffused by years of complicated, intricate life, conflict of a deep nature is bound to surface. The temptation is to try to return to simpler days. Why can't we just love each other and share with each other like we did in our early years? Can't we just discard this mess and start over with fresh love?

The answer, quite frankly, is no. We can't dismiss or deny the history we share. We cannot deny the integrity of the experiences that have led us here. At this moment, though, the cumulative effect of all our years together seems to reveal only woundedness and pain. Our hearts are filled with *if only*'s and *what if*'s. Yet we must believe that grace lies in the hidden creases and folds of our relationship. If we can just tap that grace, it will pour a healing salve over open wounds.

We cannot go back to easier days but we can (and must) surrender to a future that offers more clarity and simplicity. In surrender we finally let go of the last bits of our idealistic image of spouse. There is a realization, perhaps, that she really isn't as warm, kind and gentle as the woman you had always dreamed of marrying, or that the dream-spouse didn't have such a temper as your husband. Relinquishing the ideal image empowers full acceptance of the real other and allows grace to flow freely between you.

Surrender does not remain static and unchanging. It means full acceptance of self and other, but goes beyond. Serious conflict calls for real change. The phantoms must be discarded. In surrender, all the real players and real issues are brought to the table and sorted out with respect to the needs of each person, as well as to their needs as a couple. Surrender facilitates change.

The McDonalds move from surrender into another insightful and powerfully mature notion of love and marriage: purification.

> The struggle to surrender, as well as the search for genuine wholeness, invite a couple to enter into the fire of the purification of love. It is now clear that love is not going to go as a couple had planned it. Love has its own designs. Like all spiritualities which begin to mature, marital spirituality enters the difficult way of purification. This leads to the hidden God.

Surrender invites us into the fire of purification. This image is attractive and scary at the same time. The brave part of me romanticizes the scene. I can cross that bed of hot coals! I can climb the mountains of fire and ice—in my dreams. But the challenge is whether I can surrender to my beloved long enough to fully see her (and us) and take the necessary steps to change. This is purification in real married life.

The Spiritual Nature of Conflict

Like all powerful encounters in marriage, conflict has a spiritual nature. It reveals true self, raw need and pure emotion. These are places where God can be found. Yet it requires courage and vulnerability to go there. Why? Because I hurt now, and I've been hurting for some time, and it's only natural to protect my inner self—even from myself.

In the midst of conflict, it's not realistic for two people to share intimate spiritual growth. No, when the hurt is at its worst we are drawn separately to seek God's comfort and counsel. I may cry out in a prayer of desperation, simply seek to be held in spiritual embrace or lash out in anger at God for dealing such cards my way. The spiritual need is strong, but, oh, so solitary.

The McDonalds describe it this way:

> For many the experience of marital spirituality is simply that of staying the course, praying as best they can during hard days and believing that somehow out of the darkness, God will bring light. It is not easy. Learning to pray in the darkness represents a new experience for most of them. They stay the course and live through this stage of balancing and unbalancing simply because there is a deep intuition that it is the "right thing to do."

As the intensity of the conflict subsides and the settling benefit of my solitude and contemplation takes hold, I begin to yearn again for my beloved, gently and tentatively seeking a way to reconnect with her, to find healing and reconciliation. When talking is still impossible, I can pray— for her and for us.

Often we come together again through spiritual channels. Since we have both been in prayer and contemplation, separately but focused on the same God, we can come together in that arena to seek God's guidance through these troubled waters. In prayer and silence, we hold at bay both the irrational anger and the logical arguments designed to seal victory, and just rest in each other's presence. In that presence we discover again God's tremendous grace of love and affection.

We realize that this love experienced and shared reveals the ultimate reason why we're together and committed to each other in the first place. We cannot ignore the problems and conflicts we've set aside, of course. But tapping into the spirituality of our love—first separately and then together— gives us renewed strength to go back to the problems and hurts and find the paths to healing that were once obscured.

For Reflection and Discussion

- *How would you describe the darkest time in your marriage? Were you able to sense God's presence in that hour of darkness? If so, what was it like? What did you learn? How have you grown from enduring that experience?*

- *Would you agree that conflict and struggle are a source of spiritual growth? How has your marriage spirituality grown or changed as a result of conflict?*

CHAPTER SEVEN

Spirituality and Health

We take our health for granted until it fails us. Nobody ever caught even a cold or came down with the flu at a convenient time. We plan and organize our lives under the presumption that our bodies, our minds and our heartstrings will be humming along just fine, feeding us all the energy and vigor we need. Then—breakdown.

When illness strikes, even for just a day or two, everything gets thrown out of whack: schedules disrupted, important responsibilities ignored and vast unbudgeted funds spent on quick-relief medicines. In the meantime, "I feel so crummy. I'm sure I'm going to die. It's not just a cold this time; it's a mysterious killer virus that masks itself as severe cold symptoms."

Given enough liquids, tissues and trips to the bathroom, I slowly recover to the point where even eating is once again desirable. Now, how do I get the rest of my busy life back on track?

Taking care of myself when sick is one thing; taking care of my spouse is entirely different. "How dare she get sick now, just when I'm about to strike the deal of the century that will launch my career into outer space!" Or her reaction may be something like, "I can't believe he waits for the three-day weekend to get sick. This will ruin our plans. He never gets sick when he has to work!"

In her book *A Marriage Made in Heaven..., or, Too Tired for an Affair*, Erma Bombeck writes:

> Illness has to be one of the tests of marriage. That's why they put it in the marriage vows. Everyone sort of glides over it, but it's important. For the first time

67

you are caught naked with your pretenses down (and no makeup either). You are vulnerable and you are dependent. Neither of you married to have the other partner "take care of you." You were supposed to be a team. And now you are being seen with your head hung over a toilet bowl at 2 a.m., with another person standing over you, taking away any shred of modesty or mystique you have left.

"In sickness and in health" may be the hardest part of the marriage vows to keep. Common illnesses such as cold or flu are challenging, to be sure; but most couples have to deal at some time in their marriage with more serious health problems. Perhaps it comes as a result of a sudden accident, like what happened to Barbara.

Accidents

Chuck was on business in a town two hours from home when he got the call from the hospital. "Your wife has been in an accident. You'd better get back here as quick as you can." When he pressed for details, he learned that Barbara's legs had been crushed when a truck parked on the curb rolled into the back of Barbara's car, pinning her against it.

As Chuck rushed to the hospital, he had two predominant thoughts: "Thank God she's alive!" and "What will this mean for us now?" As it turned out, Barbara's recovery took well over a year—three surgeries and a great deal of time laid up in bed. Chuck was forced to take some leave from his job to help care for her and their three young children.

Chuck recalls:

> It was no picnic, but now I'm a much better cook than I used to be. Seriously, it was the hardest thing our family's ever been through. Hardest for Barb, of course, but all of us really lived through her injuries and recovery.
>
> How did it impact our marriage? Well, now that we can look back on the experience, we're a closer couple for having made it through this ordeal. But I'd

be lying if I said I never had any struggles or resentments during that time. There were many days when I wished I could trade places with Barb, lying up there in bed, while I was slaving away with all the housework, kids' activities, caring for her and vainly trying to keep up with my job. I was downright exhausted most of the time.

God was with us the whole time, though. That's clear to me now, but I remember right after the accident I was so angry at God for allowing this to happen to Barb and us. We certainly didn't deserve it, and quite frankly, the timing was terrible! But the whole experience bonded our family together in support for each other and in faith. An accident like Barb's is not an experience I would wish on any family, but because it happened to us, we are a more faith-full couple and family.

An accident requires a complete and immediate shift of energy and focus. The lives of couple and family are changed immediately, and the road to recovery may be months or years long. In many cases life will never be the way it was before the accident. But in most situations, recovery is a clear goal that can be attained with time, patience and perseverance. This is not always true with chronic conditions.

Chronic Illness

For the last twenty years or so, Marilee has been afflicted with a strange, chronic condition labeled *fibromyalgia*. Her husband, Frank, is her primary caretaker. Fibromyalgia is a syndrome which produces chronic pain throughout the body. Specific symptoms include constant muscle and skeletal pain, severe fatigue, muscle tenderness and great difficulty sleeping.

Nine out of ten fibromyalgia sufferers are women. Marilee experiences her chronic pain in the neck, shoulders and upper back. She has a terrible time sleeping and is always, always tired. If she feels well enough to go out for a day, it may take her three days to recover from the exertion.

As yet, there is no cure for fibromyalgia. Nor is there any effective treatment. Marilee and millions of others suffer their condition not knowing if they will ever recover.

Frank and Marilee have been married for just over thirty years. They are a fun-loving couple who have always had a lot of friends. But Marilee's condition has progressed to such a state that they cannot entertain guests anymore, and Frank has had to take early retirement in order to give more care to Marilee. She gave up on her career long ago. Yet they remain devoted to each other. Certainly they've had their struggles in marriage, but they've not wavered in their commitment. What gives them the courage and strength to carry on when there is seemingly no hope for recovery?

"Oh, we have hope," says Frank. "Without hope for an end to this struggle, we'd be completely lost. Yet we've also realized we have to embrace the life we have right here and now. Of course we wish things were different. Who wouldn't say that about some aspect of their life? We have to find true living within the life we have. And we couldn't do that without our faith and our faithful friends.

"Years ago we were active in Marriage Encounter. During that time we learned a great deal about marriage. Perhaps the two most important things we learned were to share our feelings and our faith with each other, and to make sure we have supportive friends always available to us. We certainly didn't know then how valuable, even lifesaving, those two lessons would be for us."

There is no end in sight to Marilee's condition. But through faith and friends, Frank and Marilee continue in their love and life together.

Depression

Depression often accompanies chronic physical illness. As an illness that alters one's personality, it's a tremendous challenge to a marriage.

Emily has been afflicted with low-grade clinical depression for years. Her self-esteem has never been very high. But on occasion, seemingly out of the blue, a burden of darkness forces her to retreat into herself, rendering any human interaction painful, abrasive and terribly exhausting.

There are reasons, of course, for Emily's condition. She grew up amid stormy, unstable family relationships, and she was likely verbally abused as a child. Emily has seen a counselor/therapist on and off over the years, but has resisted any psychiatric drug therapy. The periods of depression come at will and last usually a day or two, sometimes a week or longer.

Emily's husband, Jack, is very supportive of her struggles, but is often caught off-guard by her mood swings. Still, they have remained very close and loving. Emily claims that without Jack, there are times when she would see no reason for living. Yet, when she is gripped by her depression, Jack feels isolated and helpless. "It's best to leave her alone when she's really down. But then, to be honest, I worry about her getting more depressed. Sometimes I just sit with her for a long while, even if I know she'd rather I leave."

Emily and Jack cling to their faith and spirituality. They pray. They sit in silence. They search for healing. And above all else they rely on God's supportive love for them as shown through their love for each other.

They don't know what the future holds. They're not sure how they will respond if Emily's condition worsens. But they know they have each other and God to turn to.

A Spirituality of Health and Illness

How does a couple develop a spirituality of health and illness? I'm not sure, except for the fact that each of the couples mentioned above will testify that their faith and their prayer life is richer and deeper as a result of accident or illness. While many other couples may fall into despair in the face of such challenges, these couples show there is a real possibility of spiritual growth.

They bound themselves, side-by-side, to face the struggle together; like a clay pot being fired, they were strengthened by the experience. But none of them faced the problem alone. As mere humans, they quickly realized they could not cope without help. So they turned to God for support, guidance and nurture. And in the process of sickness and healing, they learned to pray—really pray.

They also learned a great deal about themselves, their unique love relationship, their stamina and perseverance, their faith and spirituality. They learned just how sacred their marriage is.

As Thomas Moore writes in his preface to *Soul Mates*:

> Relationships, I believe, are truly sacred, not in the superficial meaning of simply being high in value, but in that they call upon infinite and mysterious depths in ourselves, in our communities, and in the very nature of things.

There is a sacred nature to illness because it brings out just those qualities that Moore refers to. When one of us is ill for a prolonged period, something deeper is revealed about ourselves and our world around us. If we allow the revelation to take shape, we can occasionally glimpse our lives in the future. This may mean rearranging our priorities, moving out of a less than satisfying job or, perhaps, focusing on the two of us until we suddenly find clear, unobstructed paths to each other's heart. We find ourselves sharing at a depth hitherto unattained.

Nobody seeks out illness. It can never be pleasant. But that does not mean that being afflicted (and for most couples it's not a matter of *if* but, rather, *when*), cannot be fruitful. The challenge, of course, is responding to the demands for imagination just at a time when all your energy is focused on the illness. Yet even if we simply embrace the illness and all its ramifications amid all the pain and struggle it has caused, its sacredness and meaning for life may also be revealed.

Later in his book, Moore addresses illness directly:

> Even illness brings something of value to the soul and always, in spite of our efforts to find a cause in the temporal order, presents us with mysteries to

72

contemplate and to face emotionally.... Of course, serious illness shakes the soul even more, offering it unusually fertile material for its rumination.

Serious illness shakes the souls of the afflicted and the beloved. While none of us would ever choose to be confronted with this challenge, it cannot help but impact us at a deep spiritual level. Illness causes us to think deeper, pray with greater sincerity and look at each other with unpretentious love and consideration. When we do these things, we cannot help but be changed at our most intimate and spiritual levels.

Moore concludes by drawing an interesting parallel between the struggles of illness and the maladies of love. Both can render much pain, anguish, melancholy and need for discernment and soul-searching. Discovering and living with illness presents nothing of the rush of enthusiastic joy of discovering each other and falling in love. Moore's point is that both experiences present a ripe spiritual condition for nurturing the soul. Illness, like love, rarely fits snugly into a calm and ordered life.

Beyond Why

My wife, Rene, has dealt with chronic illness for the last ten years. Her condition is not debilitating, or anywhere near as serious as those mentioned above. Yet it is always there. And we have experienced every emotion as a result: sadness, despair, anger, depression, love, hope, joy, sorrow, melancholy, frustration and waiting, waiting, waiting....

The hardest periods for us as a couple are when she is dealing with a different emotion than I. At any given time, she may be filled with hope, while I am in despair. Or I may be feeling quietly resigned, while she is at the very end of her patience. We try to give each other permission to have different feelings and we try to express them in loving, gentle ways. We don't always succeed, but we try.

If you or your beloved has been afflicted by illness or accident, then perhaps this chapter has struck a chord with you; perhaps it has touched a raw nerve. In either case, you can certainly add your story and insights. There's no logic or fairness to illness. Why Rene and not someone else? Why now, instead of earlier or later? Why? Why? Why?

It may feel good to vent emotionally with the "why" questions, but beyond that they are of little use. With accident and/or illness, we are challenged as a couple to move beyond why and listen to the Spirit groaning in the pain of our souls.

For Reflection and Discussion

- *When your beloved is sick, does he or she want to be nursed and cared for, or to be left alone? How about yourself?*

- *Some people seem to have natural nurturing skills; others don't. When your spouse is ill, are you a good caretaker? How do you express your love and concern and care?*

- *Have the two of you ever had to deal with a serious illness or accident? How did it affect your marriage? Your spirituality? Your prayer? What did you discover about God through this experience?*

CHAPTER EIGHT

Spirituality of Parenting

How many thousands of times have you and your beloved experienced real joy and intimacy because of your children? You know what I mean. The two of you share a knowing glance, a good laugh, a long cry, a flood of memories all because together you have loved and nurtured your child. How many times did the two of you finally arrange to get away together, even if only for an afternoon or an evening, and spend the first half of your time talking about the kids? Count, if you can, the times you have thought to yourself, "Oh, I've got to remember to tell her father about that. She was just too cute!"

The depth of intimacy and spirituality found in raising a child cannot be equaled. There is no more powerful spiritual encounter available to us every single day than participating in God's creative process through our children.

OK, I know parenting is not a spiritual panacea. I know it's downright hard work most of the time. Noted parenting expert Anne Stokes echoes all of us when she says, "Parenting is exhausting!" Participating in creation comes with a heavy price. I know the bone-tired exhaustion—not to mention the confusion, anxiety and wonderment over nurturing and launching another fellow human journeyer. How many thousands of times have the two of you commiserated with and comforted each other over these daunting responsibilities?

In this chapter, I would like to share some ideas and challenges I have reflected on concerning a spirituality of parenting. (A version of these reflections first appeared in the February 1994 issue of *St. Anthony Messenger* under the title

"Can Your Kids See You're Catholic?".) Then I would like to conclude with a brief reflection on how parenting impacts our marriage and our spirituality.

Spirituality of Parenting

Take a stroll through your nearby bookstore and head for the Family/Parenting section. You'll find more advice than you could ever possibly use. There are probably more books on raising teenagers in America than there are teenagers in America. But what makes our parenting sacred? How do we filter all that advice, those skills, tips and ideas through our spiritual beliefs?

As a believer, if I relied only on spiritually-based parenting materials, the pickings would be pretty slim. Besides, a lot of the so-called secular advice makes good sense: giving children choices within proper limits; providing logical consequences rather than arbitrary punishment in response to their poor choices; maintaining my own self-esteem as a parent; giving each child a meaningful role in the ongoing operation of the family. There's no religious label on these ideas, but they've been a great help to me.

A spirituality of parenting lies not in tips and ideas, but at a deeper level of attitude and core identity. How do I allow my faith to permeate my interactions with my children? I find myself reflecting on several personal challenges in this realm.

Do I parent with faith-based values? When our children were babies, I had no trouble living the corporal works of mercy every day, right in my own home. As a parent, you've done the same: fed the hungry, clothed the naked, tended the sick and so on. These deeds are built right into parenting, so take all the spiritual credit you deserve. It's a good thing, too, because babies have a way of occupying a parent's every conscious moment—and many semi-conscious hours as well.

As babies grow into little people, expressing spiritual values becomes a different challenge. Can I see the face of Jesus in my children while they terrorize each other or when

76

they swarm around me like pesky flies at the most inopportune times or when they so effortlessly bring out the very worst in me? Do I afford my young teenager the integrity and respect due all persons even when he subjects me to his obstinate silent treatment? Can I love my children unconditionally? Can I forgive them seventy times seven times? These are core faith values. Perhaps I would succeed if they spent more time sleeping.

Once a visiting friend demonstrated in a simple way her respect for the human dignity of our children. Each time she spoke to one of them, she squatted down to their eye level. This simple gesture of demonstrated equality brought forth more maturity, kindness and social grace from our boys than any pre-visit lecture (with rewards promised for good behavior) could ever hope to accomplish.

Even though our children are younger and (in most cases) smaller than we, each is still a whole human being, deserving honor, respect and love.

Do I remember that I am simply a steward of my child's journey until she or he can steward his or her own journey? It's normal to feel self-conscious about how our children's behavior reflects on us, but too often we do more choosing for them than we should.

At a parenting session, I met an exasperated mother who was tired of helping her child get dressed each day. "He may be a little old for that, but we've got to be out of the house by eight sharp! If I don't help him get dressed, we don't make it on time. Besides, I just can't stand it when he chooses his own clothes because nothing ever matches." This mother knew things had to change, but she just didn't know how to do it. Her child was twelve years old.

Sometimes we over-parent our children. Perhaps if we shift our mindset from ownership to stewardship, our reactions will be healthier. Stewardship is an ancient term recognizing that the Creator has entrusted a work of art to someone not just for care and protection, but also for nurturance, growth and empowerment.

But how do we apply stewardship to parenting? In her book, *Gently Lead*, Polly Berrends writes:

> One thing that seems to get overlooked is that Jesus is the only person in recorded history whose parents thought he was a child of God rather than their own creative project and possession. Jesus' parents did not think he was their child. Even before he was born they said that he was a child of God. I know of no other parents in history who have from the very outset regarded their offspring as God's and not their own.

The goal of parenting is not to shape our kids into the image and likeness of us, but rather nurture them to become the true person God has created them to be. A child needs encouragement as a plant needs sun and water.

I admire the mother who admitted she was still dressing her twelve-year-old. She had the courage to name the basic struggle of "letting go" that all parents face. The group gave her some ideas, and she had good news to report at the next session. "It's amazing how quick he can be when he knows he doesn't get breakfast until he's dressed. His clothes don't always match, but I'm learning to let go. I expect his peers will take care of that problem for me real soon."

How is spirituality an expressed priority in our lives? In their study, *Secrets of Strong Families*, Nick Stinnet and John Defrane found that healthy families spend a lot of time talking with each other. They share a lot of conversation. Yet much of their communication is sharing surface information: making plans, connecting schedules and so on. But Stinnet and Defrane found that these healthy families would more readily find themselves sharing on a deeper, more intimate level. In other words, you can't get to the "quality time" without the "quantity."

The same is true in the faith arena. If faith issues are a regular part of daily activity and conversation, there is greater potential for increased religious intimacy. Everyone is more at ease, giving the Spirit more freedom to move.

How does a family do this? Try simple gestures like offering a little blessing at bedtime, telling a child that you will pray for him or her today, mentioning how you've encountered God throughout the day. If done with sincerity, these little activities will show our children that faith and spirituality have real meaning in our lives.

Do we turn to our faith to guide our decisionmaking? No parenting decision ever seems minor at the moment. We're always wondering what sort of lifelong ramifications our choices will have on our kids. Applying the filter of faith to our decisionmaking helps in several ways.

First, our common faith urges us to communicate as husband and wife, as parent and child or as a whole family about the particular dilemma. Each is challenged to set aside personal motives and look at the issue from a broader faith perspective. Not only does this make it easier to talk through the issue, it can also lead to better mutual decisions.

Second, it allows time to step back and look at the issue from a different angle. A golfer lining up a putt looks at the terrain from a variety of angles to get a clearer picture of how the ball will roll toward the hole. What's the faith-angle of the pending decision?

Third, it stimulates a concrete effort to pinpoint the spiritual values that lie at the base of the given dilemma. Some folks ask themselves how Jesus would act in this situation.

Some necessary parental decisions are not very popular with our children. Sometimes we're downright villains in the eyes of our kids. Faith may be our only friend during these times. Yet we've all heard stories about when, years later, the child comes back to say, "Thanks for making that hard choice. I know I didn't make it easy for you. But now, I'm glad you did it."

Do we forgive and reconcile with one another? If your house is like ours, forgiveness has to be the number one principle to live by. Someone is always stepping on somebody else's toes, both literally and figuratively. And we all know how children behave when they've been wronged. Somehow they don't need to be taught how to express rage.

This is when our own patterns of conflict resolution emerge. Some of us were brought up to avoid conflict at all costs, while others learned at an early age to argue loud and long. These are common patterns that children observe and learn in many households. Or they may learn the only way to deal with conflict is by hitting. These patterns may feel natural because they've been passed on from one generation to the next, but that does not make them healthy—or Christian for that matter.

Healthy families lay their problems, secrets and frustrations on the table to be addressed and reconciled. They use healthy communication patterns to state their feelings, listen to the other's response. They seek a solution rather than laying blame. And they say they're sorry over and over and over again. When these reconciliation patterns are modeled by adults, it's much easier for children to learn them.

With patience, self-control, perseverance and a genuine loss of pride, we can gently show our children the great power and reward of reconciliation.

So what makes our parenting spiritual? The answer lies more in who we are as believers than any set of particularly religious tips for better parenting. It is the foundation from which we exercise our best judgment for the guidance and care our children need. It's not a matter of "doing the Christian thing," but rather of filtering all we do as parents through a faith-based lens. If we are securely rooted in our faith, then our parenting efforts can't help but reflect that.

Parenting and Marriage Spirituality

Parenting allows us to share in the act of creation, unifying us with God, the ultimate Creator. We share God's joys, awes and sighs—and also God's frowns, frustrations and tears. On a good day, there is nothing better than reveling in parenthood. On a bad day, there are few things worse than having to claim that child as my own. Some days we look at each other and wonder out loud, "Why did we have these kids anyway?" But other times, as you know, we wouldn't trade them for all the peace and quiet of a desert island.

Parenting has been good for our marriage. Starting the day they were born, our boys have stifled many intimate moments with temper tantrums, interrupted countless conversations with inane questions, foiled outings and getaways with typical but untimely childhood sicknesses and worn us to the bone with exhaustion at the end of nearly every day. Even so, they have been a blessing in our marriage if for no other reason than they have heightened and sustained our yearning for each other's company.

If we had only the two of us, I wonder, would we make love more often? Would we take more and longer walks around the neighborhood? Would we really sustain those conversations, or allow the radio or newspaper to distract us? I'd like to think we would do all these, and some days I'd certainly like to be given the opportunity to prove it. I'm grateful to my children, though, for keeping the yearning alive between us.

But of course there's also much genuine marital fulfillment in parenting itself. We are partners on this tremendous task of nurturing and launching two fellow journeyers into the world. On the good days, we stand together and marvel at their gifts and vibrancy—and allow ourselves a little bit of credit. On less-than-stellar days, we still stand together to support, commiserate and sympathize with each other. Every day we are shown the complexity and mystery of human life. No matter how many parenting books we read or how many positive discipline theories we employ, full understanding and control always elude us. And thank God for that, because in our children lies a glimpse of the creative God who fills us with wonder and awe.

Often, when Rene and I are alone and loving and intimate, I'm just sure I can see the face of God in her eyes. When our love is full and our closeness complete, I am enveloped in God's presence. Occasionally my children also afford me such spiritual intimacy:

"Dad, do you need a hug?"
"Dad, I need to talk about something important."
"Dad, can I read you the poem I've written?"

Sometimes, the only thing between me and a son is God's precious love bonding us together. And, almost as good as the experience is telling Rene about it, because she knows exactly what I'm trying to describe. I think, perhaps, you do too.

For Reflection and Discussion

- *What are the three most important values to you in your parenting? Have you ever tried to articulate them—actually write them down? If asked, would your children name these same values?*

- *How could you exercise more "stewardship" and less "ownership" in your parenting?*

- *How could your family turn to faith or apply a spiritual lens to your family decisionmaking? Is there a looming decision that needs to be prayed over?*

- *How has parenting both enriched and challenged your marriage? Your spirituality as a couple?*

CHAPTER NINE

Work, Career, Vocation and Spirituality

For some, work is fulfilling. To work is to contribute to the fabric of human existence. Even in the most mundane tasks, many workers revel in contributing to the big picture of accomplishment. Plus, they enjoy the satisfaction of "putting in a day" on the job, earning an income, supporting themselves and perhaps a family and just enjoying that good tired feeling at the end of the day.

For many, this rush of satisfaction via labor and accomplishment is addictive and often detrimental to marriage and family. Without Rene's gentle but constant insistence on balance, I would likely be well down that road to workaholism. I have held some kind of job since I was twelve, and have always enjoyed digging in and getting a job done (although plumbing problems around the house are not my forte). Rene, on the other hand, has never taken much interest in employment. Make no mistake, her ability and energy to labor goes unquestioned. She just doesn't care for the rat race of the working world. She instinctively knows how to balance labor with rest and leisure. I envy her.

A lot of work, of course, has nothing to do with employment. Much unpaid labor goes into maintaining one's life and household. You know these jobs: cleaning, cooking, yard work, parenting, gardening, shuttling kids and so on. Here is where the two of us toil together, and perhaps the hardest.

How can work and career remain a source of esteem and growth without becoming the sole source? How do we keep it from enveloping our lives? For many (including myself), this is an ongoing challenge of balancing the rush and satisfaction of work achievement with the relational responsibilities of marriage and home life.

Many find it easier to "succeed" at work than at home. For one thing, it's easier to know what success is on the job than at home or in marriage. Many, therefore, slip into spending more time and their best energy at work.

Others keep their work in balance. They realize the necessity and benefits of employment, but they arrange their workload and expectations to reflect that the job is not the most important thing in their lives.

Work Versus Marriage

Don's job is demanding and family finances dictate his long hours. For the last three months he's been working even harder and longer than usual. Success with his special project could mean a nice promotion and greater financial security. "Don't worry, dear," Don says to his wife, Helen. "As soon as this project is complete things will ease off and return to normal."

The best Helen can do is nod with a sad expression. After hearing this line over and over for the last ten years, she wonders when it was ever "normal." Meanwhile the kids are fighting again.

Job concerns can drive a wedge into a marriage, moving two lovers apart. We live in a culture that rewards doing more than being. The more we do, the more we accomplish, the more accolades (and money) we get. We are a society addicted to production. We have lost a sense of balance between work and relationship to such an extent that many people's primary relationship is to their job.

There was a time in our history when there was little or no separation between home and work (as is still true in some parts of the world today). Work was done at home—on the farm or in the small community—and all family members contributed in meaningful ways. Work was a communal partnership that all participated in. Rather than dividing a family, it provided a unifying factor. There was a healthy balance between the roles of producer and consumer.

While the line between work and home became blurred or even nonexistent, the social boundary protecting marriage and family from the ills of society remained sound and healthy. As families worked, lived and loved together in the same place, they held onto all the major functions of healthy human growth. The family had primary responsibility and ultimate control over education, health care, spiritual formation, recreation and, of course, emotional nurturing. The rest of society played a secondary role in supporting the family in these crucial tasks.

Society today has turned the tables. First, we have separated producers from consumers and, more importantly, separated family life from work life. Perhaps the greatest cause of fragmentation of marriage and family has been a work system separate from home, primarily male-dominated and ultimately focused on short-term success.

In addition, the healthy, protective separation between the home and society has nearly vanished. Social institutions have supplanted most of the family functions mentioned above. We typically receive our primary health care from a highly bureaucratized health maintenance organization; if you see the same physician twice in a year's time it may be pure happenstance. We send our children to schools for their education and to religious education class for spirituality. We enroll them in soccer, Scouts, T-ball, tap class, ballet, volleyball, summer camp, basketball, 4-H and so on to round out their recreational, social and athletic formation.

It's not that all these institutions are bad; it's just that many do not maintain a mutual working partnership with the very families they were designed to assist. Think about it. When last was sports practice or dance class not held during the dinner hour? Is that family-friendly?

Electronic media also blur the boundary between home and society. Today's American home is wired not just for TV and radio, but also for computer, video games, Internet, cable programming, direct TV and, soon, video on demand. The influence of society is readily accessible without leaving one's desk or easy chair. I heard recently that you can even order fruits and vegetables through an on-line service. Which key do I hit to thump the cantaloupe?

The media will find a way into our homes, no question. How do we as family members deal with this critically and objectively?

The separation of work from marriage and family life is directly linked to the blurring of boundaries between home life and society. While this surely has an impact on family life, it also sends subtle shock waves into many marriages. Extreme pressure to produce, accomplish and succeed can only be detrimental to a happy marriage.

Suzanne started her own small business from the basement of her house. It was actually her hobby: writing storybooks for children. Apparently she weaves a nice yarn and has business savvy, for her hobby has turned into more than a full-time job. She and a friend publish children's resources that are sold all over the country. The problem: It's become a ten-hour-a-day hobby. She's doing what she loves, and even making some money—but her husband has become rather quiet and sullen.

Spirituality of Work

What we need is a spirituality of work that is compatible with our marriage and home life. In her article, "Toward a Spirituality of Work" (*The Catholic World*, July-August, 1994), Elizabeth Dreyer writes:

> Unfortunately, work has been yet another victim of our tendency to ghettoize the holy—limiting it to deserts, caves, monasteries, convents, churches and rectories. But of course the locus of God's revealing Self-gift is not restricted, and it is time for us to wake up to the potential holiness of the office, the union meeting, city streets, the classroom and the assembly line.

And I would add to her list, the laundry room, kitchen, garage, backyard and so on. Dreyer continues:

> Along with all the other aspects of everyday living, the experience of work has the potential to become a significant locus for the revelation of God. How can work—whether uplifting or boring—be an integral part of one's journey toward holiness?

God is often revealed in my work, but I don't realize it until I have talked it through with Rene. For example, I spent months complaining about the poor management and bureaucracy of my previous position, but it was through serious, prayerful conversation with Rene that I became aware that God was calling me to change. It was more than just deciding to leave that job; the grace lay in the discovery of a new call.

The change we chose, to become self-employed, is a risky one. Indeed, the independent ministry specialist in Catholic Church circles does not encounter what you might call a lucrative market. Yet, the more we discussed it and played out the options, the clearer the choice became.

Rene has been God's messenger of encouragement and confidence. You see, usually she is the skeptic and I'm the idealist.

She usually dwells on the worst possible scenario, while I'm glossing over the details and saying, "I'm sure we can make this work. Just have faith." But it was just the opposite in this case. Rene proclaimed her strong confidence that this project would work, while I was checking and rechecking the proposed budget. "And if it doesn't work," she said, "you can always just go get a job." Easier said than done, but the strength of her faith was (and is) tremendously encouraging.

God is indeed present and active in the world of work. The job is not always a villain. As in other marriage arenas though, we need to reflect on and communicate with each other about our jobs and career ambitions. Only in an atmosphere of reflection and discussion can we discover a sense of vocation amid the demands, frustrations and satisfactions of work.

Vocation

With respect to work and career, to what, if any of this, am I "called"? Think for a moment and bring to mind one person in your life who genuinely inspires you—not necessarily a famous person, but someone you know personally.

I am thinking of a long-ago friend who recently wandered back into my life. He literally showed up at our doorstep one evening and we talked well into the night. While running a traveling carnival (not to mention the life-style) is completely foreign to me, his gift for storytelling leaves me spellbound. All of life comes alive through his romantic eyes, and you can't help but get caught up in it! He transforms me with his simple wisdom.

Does he have a vocation? Of course. Just as your inspiring person does.

Having a vocation means cooperating with God's work in the world, finding a purpose for being in the world that is related to God's purposes. Vocation is a call to partnership with God on behalf of our neighbor. (Sometimes our neighbor sleeps in the next room or even on the other side of the bed.)

Occasionally you hear someone refer to his or her vocation without realizing it. "I guess it's my calling in life to endure parenthood." I heard this comment recently from a truly gifted and wonderful mother, and I wanted to respond, "No, it's clear to me that your calling is to be an inspirational steward of your child's journey until she is ready to steward her own."

How would you describe your vocation? This is by no means an easy question. One's vocation comes from deep within, but is often more clearly seen and discerned by others. This sounds like a paradox, but it actually makes sense. If your vocation is expressed in how you make a difference in the world, then those who have benefited from your vocation will likely recognize it before you do.

Chances are your beloved can name and describe your

vocation as well or better than you can. The recipient of your love and your gifts knows how you share God's work.

Vocation does not equate only with job, work, occupation or even avocation, though you may hear it expressed that way. A middle-aged woman said, "For years, gardening has been my love. It's my release from life's stresses. Funny, I never thought I'd write a book about it. But I did!" To which I responded, "Yes, and through your book you share far greater riches than gardening skills and tips. You give us a glimpse of peace and harmony as well."

Someone speaking of a career might say, "I've worked hard shaping my career and I'm proud of what I've accomplished." The appropriate reply could be, "No one could have done what you have done in your field, but your greatest accomplishment has been showing us success with integrity and grace."

While vocation is certainly manifest in these things, it is much richer and deeper. Vocation is more closely tied to our active identity. It is our response to the invitation to partnership with God. It involves our work, to be sure, but also our leisure, our relationships and our resources put at the disposal of God's purposes.

Coming to grips with one's vocation may sound burdensome, but actually it can be quite compelling and freeing. The excellence we are called to in our vocation is never based on competition with others. Each person is singularly and uniquely gifted, and it is exactly those gifts which God calls us to use for the benefit of others. There is no shortage of ways to be a partner with God.

Consequently, we are truly free to rejoice in the unique gifts and graces of others. An added benefit here is that we are freed from the false constraints of having to be all things to all people. When you know your gifts for the sake of others, you also become comfortable with your limitations.

Vocation, then, is the opposite of workaholism. We are free to seek a reasonable balance between work and leisure. In our vocation we are freed from the tyranny of time.

Marriage Supports My Vocation

Marriage itself is a vocation. But within my marriage, I am supported and uplifted to maintain my partnership with God's purposes. My day-to-day labor, my career and my vocation are all wrapped up together, leading me down the road of meaning and purpose in life. I presume that God, the source of all meaning and purpose, can be found down this road, and so nearly every day, I journey further.

Vocation lends real meaning to my daily work and my career, and my beloved offers me the support, accountability and balance I need to pursue my vocation. I like to think I do the same for her. In our mutual support for each other, all the work we do—whether paid or unpaid, whether for others or for ourselves, whether exciting or mundane, whether productive or not—makes sense.

Dreyer concludes her article with these wistful questions.

> What if the act of work, whatever its nature, were seen as a creative act in union with the Creator, that actually builds up the earth and helps form a new human family? What if all this toil and labor were viewed as very concrete ways to continue the redemptive activity of Jesus, a specific mode of dying and rising with him? What if the spiritual lives of millions of Christians were expanded to include their whole lives, including the daily round of work? What if?

For Reflection and Discussion

- *What kinds of labor do you engage in that you consider truly meaningful, perhaps even redemptive?*

- *How would you describe your personal vocation? How do you cooperate with and participate in God's work in the world?*

- *How would your beloved describe your vocation?*

CHAPTER TEN

Must We Always Be So Serious?

Several years ago I found Rene on our bedroom floor, stretching. She was doing a series of yoga postures. I was amazed that she could twist her body into so many different positions. A person of some athletic prowess raised in a competitive atmosphere, I was compelled to show her that I can do anything she can—only better. So I got down on the floor and began to copy her movements and postures.

Before long the little grin on her face turn into giggles and then outright laughter. I was grunting and groaning, trying to force my legs and arms to do what hers could do. When she offered several hints to make it easier, I nodded, but my pride wouldn't let me succumb to her leadership. Within twenty minutes I was in a heap on the floor. And Rene was smugly satisfied in besting her "athletic" husband.

"Let me show you some basic postures," she said. "Nobody can do advanced yoga right at first." As foolish as I felt, I consented. This was the beginning of a wonderful period in our marriage: exercising together.

I discovered I really enjoyed yoga, and before long was doing rather well at it. But more beneficial was the experience of doing something new and different together. Along with becoming more healthy through yoga, we've also grown closer to each other, thanks to God's playful grace.

I'm the kind of person who normally chooses work over play. I have trouble enjoying myself if there are still unchecked items on my to-do list. But I know that leisure, play and fun are necessary for balance in my life. I need to relax more, take on fewer tasks, be more open to new and intriguing activities. If I don't pursue more leisure in my life, I'm afraid I'll turn out to be a grouchy old man with relatively few interests and even fewer friends.

I know, too, that if Rene and I don't play together we endanger the quality of our relationship. Not only that, we also lose an arena in which to grow closer to God.

Knowing all this is one thing. Living it is another.

Up to now, the chapters in this book have been pretty serious. Marriage and family living, while spiced with many joys and moments of laughter, cannot be taken lightly in our society. But there is a difference between serious and sober.

Some of us too easily lose our spontaneity and our capacity for fun. What do the two of you do to relax and enjoy each other? How do you make time for these activities on a regular basis?

One couple I know has had a standing Saturday night date for their entire twenty-odd years of marriage. They don't normally go for pricey nights out. They are content with a simple dinner, a movie, perhaps a special lecture or a long walk in the park on a summer evening. They want and need their couple-time. What they do is not so important as just enjoying each other's company.

When their children were babies, they were tempted to forego their Saturday nights for the sake of the kids. "A sitter can't possibly care for our babies like we can," they reasoned. True enough, but a trusted sitter won't cause any great harm in a couple of hours. Meanwhile, time out of the house, away from the demands of little ones, not only replenished their relationship but also recharged their parenting energies.

Rene and I take a walk around the neighborhood nearly every day. Thirty or forty minutes at the end of the day brings us in touch with each other, offers mutual commiseration over the struggles of the day and helps us remember that we're both on the same team. If our boys would just prepare supper while we're out walking, we'd have it made!

In his book, *Your Family in Focus: Appreciating What You Have and Making It Even Better*, Mitch Finley writes, "Healthy marriage requires time. Someone once said that a marriage is like a little child, it needs to be picked up and hugged and given plenty of tender loving care."

Mary and Dennis have three young children (eight, six and three), so they don't have the luxury of taking a nightly walk. They value their time after the kids are in bed, though. Dennis says, "We're pretty strict with bedtime in the evening. The kids need their sleep, of course, but Mary and I need our time too."

Once the kids are down, Mary and Dennis like to curl up in each other's arms and watch a video, or make popcorn and visit, or even just sit quietly and read together. Once or twice a year, they get away for an overnight—just the two of them.

If couples don't spend their time and money on themselves, why be married?

Not So Simple

It's not always so simple, is it? Life is filled with complicated circumstances that cause us to compromise even our best intentions. We relinquish control to many things; job, school, kids' activities, car or house problems and so on.

In addition to these externals, the timing between two spouses may be off. You may arrive at a conviction that you really need to spend more fun time together. This marriage needs some fresh air, some new blood and a new "exercise" routine. But your beloved may not be on the same page with you. He or she may be feeling the need for more personal time; or, while what you propose sounds good in theory, he or she just doesn't have the same energy for it.

The couples mentioned above have experienced this struggle, but they have moved beyond the feelings of the moment and established couple time as a priority. They don't ignore all the other issues; they just don't allow their time together to be ignored either.

Back in the early days of courtship and honeymoon, it seemed easy to spontaneously take in a movie, go for an afternoon hike in the woods, see a play or whatever. But now, if it doesn't get planned into the schedule, too often it doesn't happen.

In their book *Promises to Keep: Developing the Skills of Marriage*, Thomas H. Hart and Kathleen Fischer encourage couples to "[find] the fun in it all." They preface their ideas with these comments:

> In marriage, as in life, there must be times of rest and play. A walk along a lake, a game of volleyball, sharing a meal out—these all nourish a marriage relationship as much as developing communication skills and learning to resolve differences. Married intimacy is deepened by moments of shared wonder at the beauty of a winter sunset or the first spring buds on bushes and trees, by times of mutual excitement over a piece of music or a painting. In fact, when things aren't going well, it may be a sign that we need to lighten up and have more fun together.

Fischer and Hart offer several practical suggestions.

Develop new interests and activities. When's the last time the two of you tried something totally new and different? How about yoga? Or going out for East Indian food, taking up square-dancing, volunteering with your church or a social service agency? I have friends who have tried all of these things, and it gives them something new to talk about and look forward to.

Celebrate special times together. Birthdays, anniversaries and other occasions provide ample opportunity to celebrate. When was the last surprise party you gave for your beloved's birthday? For several years, Rene and I have hosted a charades party on Valentine's Day. Each couple mimes a title related to love and romance. I'm a reluctant and lousy charades player, but those parties were great fun. We know another couple who host an Academy Awards party every year. Guests come dressed as their favorite movie character.

Feed the humor in your relationship. Fischer and Hart ask, "What frees up the child in your relationship, and shows you the crazy and delightful sides of each other? Nobody can escape the work component of marriage. It would be a shame if the play component got crowded out."

Some couples tease each other and develop a language of humor that only they can understand and appreciate. They banter back and forth with "outrageous" statements and language that is solely their own: "So that's the real reason you married me!" "I knew I'd be happier with a younger man." Sometimes just a glance or facial expression carries a humorous message that requires no explanation. When the two of us have a "language" all our own, it spices the daily routine and shows that we can generate our own enjoyment just from being together.

A Spirituality of Play

It's easy to find fault and failing in each other, and perhaps to get stuck there. I know a man who always complains about his wife; any and every thing she does or doesn't do seems to bother him. Yet if you knew his wife, you would be hard pressed to see why he complains so much.

The call of marriage, though, is to find the joy and surprise in our relationship. The opening invocation of the Episcopal marriage rite includes the phrase, "The union of husband and wife in heart, body and mind is intended by God for their mutual joy."

There it is in black and white! It is actually God's intention that we experience real and mutual joy in being married to each other. As believers, we must heed God's call to ferret out the fun, laughter and joy amid the many opportunities to quarrel and struggle with each other.

Here's a quick quiz to test your knowledge of the Gospels. What Gospel story do we most often cite to validate and uphold the sacramental nature of marriage? What story shows that marriage is a legitimate vocational call? Answer: the wedding feast at Cana (John 2:1-10)! You remember the story: Mary and Jesus went to a wedding. The wine was running low and, to save embarrassment, Mary turned to

Jesus. Reluctantly, he turned several barrels of water into wine so the party could continue.

If theologians and Scripture scholars can use this story to stress the sacramental nature of marriage (even though we never meet the bride or groom), we can also use it to support a spirituality of celebration! Even a decidedly amateur Scripture scholar like myself can interpret from this story the spiritual value of feasting and celebrating. The miracle was not so much turning water into wine, but rather in not allowing the party to end prematurely. We all need to relax and let loose once in a while. Mary understood this, so she turned to Jesus for help.

I believe we can safely conclude that not only is leisure, fun and party good for marriage, it's also good for spiritual growth. Just as we may become a bit too sober in marriage, we are perhaps even more so with our spirituality. Let's lighten up, enjoy each other and open up to the playfulness and intoxication of the Spirit. You never know where God's grace may explode!

For Reflection and Discussion

- *What do the two of you do to relax and have fun together? How long has it been since you last did it?*

- *When was the last time the two of you tried something totally new and different?*

- *Discuss with your spouse how you encounter God in your play. What are the similarities and differences between the two of you? What could you do together to enjoy the "playfulness and intoxication of the Spirit"?*

Conclusion

The spiritual journey is not reserved for monks, mystics and monastics. God's gracious presence lingers with all of us. The essence of spirituality is presence. The same is true for relationships. We simply cannot sustain our marital love without choosing to be fully present to one another. Likewise, we cannot grow in our spiritual life without seeing and responding to God's loving presence.

Fortunately, there are many times when our presence to each other—as lovers, best friends, partners—also affords the opportunity to tap the presence of the Spirit. A spirituality of marriage reveals God's grace in the very essence of our lives together. God can be found in our lovemaking, our partnering, our fighting, our parenting, our illnesses, our work and our play. Place the emphasis on *our*. In whatever is ours, God is there and eager to be discovered. The journey of true love feeds and sustains the journey of faith, and vice versa.

Spirituality is a need, along with relationships and love. By wonderful divine design we can, in marriage, meet these needs for each other and grow to greater heights and deeper intimacy than we ever imagined.

May God bless the two of you on your spiritual journey.

For Further Reading

Anderson, Herbert and Robert Cotton Fite. *Becoming Married* (Louisville, Ky.: Westminster/John Knox Press, 1993). This book examines issues surrounding the process of forming the marriage bond: courtship, early years and the events that must take place for successful bonding to occur.

Dominian, Jack. *Dynamics of Marriage* (Mystic, Conn.: Twenty-Third Publications, 1993). An honest, unsparing and, yet, ultimately hopeful look at the possibility of true Christian marriage in contemporary society.

Genovesi, Vincent J. *In Pursuit of Love: Catholic Morality and Human Sexuality* (Wilmington, Del.: Michael Glazier, 1987). A thorough and balanced presentation of sexual morality with a helpful pastoral tone.

Hart, Thomas H., and Kathleen R. Fischer. *Promises to Keep: Developing the Skills of Marriage* (Mahwah, N.J.: Paulist Press, 1991). A practical, easy-to-read book addressing the everyday issues of marriage in the context of faith and spirituality.

Mackin, Theodore. *What is Marriage?: Marriage in the Catholic Church* (Mahwah, N.J.: Paulist Press, 1982). A comprehensive book covering the development of the theology and Christian understanding of marriage. An excellent historical resource.

McDonald, Patrick J. and Claudette M. *The Soul of a Marriage* (Mahwah, N.J.: Paulist Press, 1995). An excellent book covering the struggles and the darker side of marriage. Good practical examples that all can relate to.

Lawler, Michael G. *Marriage and Sacrament: A Theology of Christian Marriage* (Collegeville, Minn.: The Liturgical Press, 1993). An excellent resource on the theology of Christian marriage. Good treatment of the historical development of the sacrament.

Oliver, Mary Anne McPherson. *Conjugal Spirituality: The Primacy of Mutual Love in Christian Tradition* (Kansas City, Mo.: Sheed and Ward, 1994). An insightful treatment of marital spirituality. Nice chapter on couple exercises and rituals.

Roberts, William P. *Marriage: Sacrament of Hope and Challenge* (Dayton, Ohio: University of Dayton Bookstore, 1996). A practical application of the sacramental nature of marriage. Offers helpful insight into scriptural references to marriage.

St. Romain, Phillip and Lisa Bellecci. *Living Together, Loving Together: A Spiritual Guide to Marriage* (Liguori, Mo.: Liguori, 1995). A practical reflection on the "skills" of marriage from a spiritual/Christian viewpoint. Lots of practical exercises and dialogue questions.

Thomas, David M. *Written on Scrolls, Inscribed in Hearts: Biblical Reflections on Marriage* (St. Meinrad, Ind.: Abbey Press, 1989). A nice look at marriage from a biblical perspective, written in an easy-to-read manner. The reader does not have to be a Scripture scholar to enjoy this book.

Tomonto, Bob and Irene, and Myrna Gallagher. *The Covenant Experience: Eleven Steps to a Better Marriage* (San Jose, Calif.: Resource Publications, 1995). This is a book of exercises to enhance marriage and spirituality.

Whitehead, Evelyn Eaton and James D. *Marrying Well: Stages on the Journey of Christian Marriage* (Garden City, N.Y.: Image Books, 1983). A comprehensive look at marriage from a Christian perspective. This is perhaps the best book for linking the human experience with the spirituality and sacramentality of marriage.

_____. *A Sense of Sexuality: Christian Love and Intimacy* (New York: Doubleday, 1989). An inspiring treatment of sexuality and intimacy from a healthy Christian perspective.